MORE GOOD FOOD

ANNEKA MANNING

PRAISE FOR *GOOD FOOD*

'When the history of food in late 20th century Australia is written, it may well emerge that one of the greatest influences on the Australian diet was *australian good taste* magazine...
Now *good taste* magazine is also a book, *good food* has the stylish sensibilities of the glossies without any of their airs and graces. It offers sensible, accessible, approachable recipes that are thoroughly modern but which wouldn't scare anyone.'

STEPHANIE WOOD, *AGE*

'Intelligent, friendly and guaranteed to drive even half-hearted cooks into the kitchen.'

SYDNEY MORNING HERALD

'*good food* has a wonderful diversity of recipes, focusing on fresh seasonal produce. The book is strengthened by the information Anneka Manning delivers outside the recipes—for storage of fruit, vegetables or herbs, for microwave usage, for seasonal produce shopping and for preparation.'

HIGH COUNTRY LIVING

'If you don't flick through this book and find at least 10 things you want to eat immediately, well, you probably aren't that hungry. But it's a gorgeous compendium of recipes, photographed simply as we've come to expect from the magazine that spawned it.'

SUNDAY AGE

'These inspirational recipes make use of widely available ingredients. This is "no tricks" food— what you see is what you get. And that of course is what good food is all about.'

NINETOFIVE

'At last! The cookbook you've been waiting for. *good food* by Anneka Manning is a gorgeous cookbook offering simple and seasonally based recipes that you will want to cook again and again.'

CHRONICLE

MORE
GOOD FOOD

ANNEKA MANNING

TEXT PUBLISHING
MELBOURNE AUSTRALIA

Anneka Manning was born in Cooma, New South Wales, in 1970.
She has been food editor of *australian good taste* magazine
since its inception in July 1996 and is also the author of *good food*.

The Text Publishing Company
171 La Trobe Street
Melbourne Victoria 3000
Australia

First published in 2000
Printed by australian book connection
Designed by Yolande Gray
Typeset in Sabon 9/15

National Library of Australia
Cataloguing-in-Publication data:
Manning, Anneka, 1970-.
More good food.
Includes index.
ISBN 1 876485 56 6.
1. Cookery. I. Title.
641.5

Some of the material in this book has previously been published in *australian good taste*.

AUTHOR
Anneka Manning

RECIPE COORDINATOR
Michelle Lawton

ART DIRECTOR
Yolande Gray

PHOTOGRAPHER
William Meppem

STYLIST
Amber Keller

EDITOR
Anna Scobie

DRINKS CONSULTANT
Stuart Gregor

MICROWAVE CONSULTANT
Janelle Bloom

FOOD PHOTOGRAPHY ASSISTANTS
Kerrie Mullins; Michelle Lawton

cover: spiced caramelised oranges with mascarpone cream (page 70)

note: all recipes are tested with 59/60g eggs. All recipes are tested in conventional
ovens. For fan-forced temperatures and times, contact your oven's manufacturer.

CONTENTS

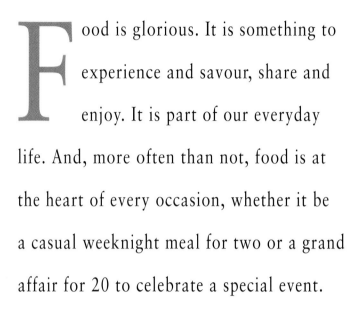

Food is glorious. It is something to experience and savour, share and enjoy. It is part of our everyday life. And, more often than not, food is at the heart of every occasion, whether it be a casual weeknight meal for two or a grand affair for 20 to celebrate a special event.

More than a recipe book, *more good food* is about sharing an unforgettable aroma, a delicious flavour, and a friendly table. It is a companion to guide, inform and inspire. *more good food* will help you make every occasion a memorable one. The recipes are clear and simple with uncomplicated preparation and straightforward cooking instructions. The flavour combinations may be familiar

or new, but I can promise all will please. For ease of use, the recipes have been compiled into menus designed to take the stress out of planning and cooking a meal. Whether it be for one, two, four, six, eight, ten or 20, you'll be safe in the knowledge that you'll get perfect results every time.

In planning the menus, I made sure the dishes sitting side-by-side worked together. Flavours, textures and cooking techniques should be complementary but still have a certain amount of contrast to hold interest. The flow from one dish to the next should be smooth and, as the meal progresses, build a pleasurable experience. All the menus in this book have these qualities.

Although the recipes in this book have been arranged into menus, you also have the flexibility of picking and choosing, and mixing and matching. You can use individual recipes from different menus to create a combination of your own. You may even like to incorporate an old favourite.

At the start of each menu, I have suggested a suitable season. This is when the fresh ingredients will be at their best and, quite often, their cheapest. It also reflects the style of recipes. But it doesn't necessarily mean the recipes have to be restricted to this season. Many ingredients are available for more than a three-month period and, if that's the case, go for it!

To complete the menus, Stuart Gregor has made wine suggestions, so you can plan a complete dining experience. There is also a simple, no-fuss guide to matching wine with food at the end of the book to help you through the 'which wine to choose?' maze.

If you haven't already guessed, food is my passion, and I believe it is enjoyed most when it is shared. *more good food* is what I would like to share with you.

Happy cooking!

Anneka Manning

WEEKNIGHTS

Time is precious during the week and there is no room for dull-tasting food. Evening meals need to be easy, speedy, healthy and, above all, delicious. An all-in-one dish, like a stir-fry or pasta, is perfect. So, too, are risotto from the microwave, roasted lamb and vegetables for two, and fish fillets simmered in a fresh tomato sauce.

Whether for relaxed everyday eating with the family or casual entertaining on a weeknight, these recipes will make your task a breeze. They are fresh, simple and ideal when time is of the essence.

summer menu for four

CHICKEN & SPINACH BURGERS

RASPBERRY PARFAIT

*A flavoursome chardonnay
would be ideal, like Russet Ridge or Wynns,
both from Coonawarra in South Australia*

LITE & LUSCIOUS

If you don't tell them, nobody will ever guess this menu is low-fat—I have fooled many before. It's time to tuck in, without worrying about the 'bottom' line!

CHICKEN & SPINACH BURGERS

serves: 4   prep: 15–20 mins   cooking: 15–20 mins

½   bunch English spinach, washed, dried
500g   minced chicken breast fillets
25g   (¼ cup) dried (packaged) breadcrumbs
60ml   (¼ cup) reduced-fat milk
1   egg
6   green shallots, trimmed, finely chopped
1 tbs   sun-dried tomato paste
1 tbs   drained capers, finely chopped
1   small fresh red chilli, deseeded, finely chopped
   Salt & ground black pepper, to taste
1   loaf Turkish bread (about 30cm)
100g   low-fat hummus

1   Cut the stems from the spinach leaves and discard. Finely chop 8 large (about 50g) spinach leaves. Place in a medium bowl with the minced chicken, breadcrumbs, milk, egg, green shallots, tomato paste, capers and chilli. Season well with salt and pepper, and mix to combine.

2   Preheat grill on high. Press the chicken mixture evenly over the base of a 25cm (base measurement) non-stick frying pan. Cook over medium heat for 5–6 minutes or until cooked halfway through.

3   Place the pan under preheated grill and cook for 6–7 minutes or until the chicken patty is golden and just cooked through. Cut the patty into 8 wedges while still in the pan, then cover the pan with foil to keep warm.

4   Cut the bread crossways into 4 even portions, then split each portion in half horizontally. Toast the bread under preheated grill for 1–2 minutes each side or until golden.

5   To serve, top the bread bases with the remaining spinach leaves and 2 chicken wedges each. Spoon the hummus over and cover with the top half of the bread.

nutritional information per serving: 44g protein, 13g fat, 66g carbohydrate, 6g dietary fibre, 2,340kJ (560 Cals).

RASPBERRY PARFAIT

serves: 4   prep: 10 mins (+ 20 mins standing time)

80ml   (⅓ cup) orange liqueur (like Cointreau)
80ml   (⅓ cup) fresh orange juice
4   125g containers French Vanilla Light Frûche
16   Italian shortbread
200g   (1 punnet) fresh raspberries

1   Combine the liqueur and orange juice in a small jug.

2   Divide a third of the Frûche among 4 serving glasses. Break 8 shortbread into small pieces and place on top. Drizzle with half the orange juice mixture and top with half the raspberries. Repeat with half the remaining Frûche, 8 shortbread and then the remaining orange juice mixture and raspberries. Finish with the remaining Frûche.

3   Set aside for 20 minutes to let the flavours develop before serving.

nutritional information per serving: 14g protein, 8g fat, 61g carbohydrate, 3g dietary fibre, 1,850kJ (440 Cals).

ROAST LAMB WITH ROSEMARY POTATOES & GARLIC BEANS

Lamb equals cabernet sauvignon, and cabernet sauvignon equals Coonawarra—Rymill Coonawarra or Redman could be the perfect answer

ALL IN ONE

I adore roast lamb—for its flavour and ease of preparation. Throw it in the oven with garlic, rosemary and potatoes, and let it do its thing.

ROAST LAMB WITH ROSEMARY POTATOES & GARLIC BEANS

serves: 2   prep: 10 mins   cooking: 40 mins

Olive oil, for greasing

1   small (about 250g) orange sweet potato (kumara), unpeeled, cut into 1cm-thick slices

2   small (about 250g) desiree potatoes, unpeeled, cut into 1cm-thick slices

4   garlic cloves, unpeeled

2 tsp   fresh rosemary leaves

60ml   (¼ cup) olive oil

Salt & ground black pepper, to taste

1   rack of lamb (with 6 cutlets), excess fat trimmed

150g   green beans, topped

Lemon wedges (optional), to serve

1   Preheat oven to 200°C. Brush a large roasting pan with oil to grease.

2   Place the potatoes, garlic, half the rosemary, half the oil, salt and pepper in a bowl. Toss the potatoes to coat, then spread over the base of the greased pan. Roast the potatoes in preheated oven for 10 minutes or until they just begin to colour.

3   Brush the lamb with 2 tsp of remaining oil, sprinkle with remaining rosemary and season with salt and pepper. Place on top of the potatoes and roast for 25 minutes for medium or until cooked to your liking.

4   Remove pan from oven and transfer the garlic cloves to a chopping board. Cover the pan loosely with foil to keep warm and set aside.

5   Remove the skins from the garlic and roughly chop the flesh. Bring a medium saucepan of water to the boil. Add the beans and cook for 1 minute or until bright green and tender crisp. (See microwave tip.) Drain. Heat the remaining 1 tbs oil in a large frying pan over medium heat. Add the garlic and stir for 30 seconds or until aromatic. Add the beans and toss to coat. Season with salt and pepper.

6   Cut the rack of lamb in half. Divide the potatoes between serving plates and place the lamb on top. Serve with the garlic beans and lemon wedges, if desired.

microwave tip: wash the beans, place in a freezer bag and twist the opening to secure. Cook on High/800watts/100% for 1½–2 minutes or until bright green and tender crisp.

summer menu for four

LETTUCE WRAPS

SNAPPER WITH FRESH
TOMATO & BASIL SAUCE

CRUSTY BREAD

*Crisp, fresh riesling from the
Clare Valley in South Australia would be
perfect—try the likes of Taylors or
Leasingham*

A FRESH
APPROACH

*Low in fat and sugar, this menu is perfect
for those with diabetes. But don't let
them keep it to themselves—it is simply
too good for that!*

LETTUCE WRAPS

serves: 4   prep: 15 mins

8 large butter lettuce leaves, washed, dried
2 large Lebanese cucumbers, halved, cut into thin sticks
2 carrots, peeled, halved, cut into thin sticks
1 red capsicum, quartered, deseeded,
   cut into thin strips
85g (1½ cups) bean sprouts
¾ cup fresh coriander leaves
¾ cup fresh mint leaves
2 limes, juiced
1½ tbs sweet chilli sauce
   Salt & ground black pepper, to taste
   Lime wedges, to serve

1 Place 2 lettuce leaves on each serving plate. Top with the cucumber, carrots, capsicum, bean sprouts, coriander and mint.
2 Drizzle the vegetables with the lime juice and sweet chilli sauce, then season with salt and pepper. Serve with the lime wedges to squeeze over the vegetables, if desired. To eat, wrap the lettuce around the vegetables to enclose, and hold together with your fingers.

nutritional information per serving: 4g protein, 1g fat, 9g carbohydrate, 6g dietary fibre, 250kJ (60 Cals).

SNAPPER WITH FRESH TOMATO & BASIL SAUCE

serves: 4   prep: 20 mins   cooking: 15–20 mins

8 ripe tomatoes
1 tbs olive oil
2 garlic cloves, finely chopped
1 bunch green shallots, trimmed, sliced
125ml (½ cup) fish or vegetable stock
1 bay leaf
1 tsp sugar
4 (about 160g each) snapper fillets
½ cup loosely packed fresh basil leaves, torn
   Salt & ground black pepper, to taste
   Crusty bread, to serve

1 Cut a shallow cross in the base of each tomato and place in a large heatproof bowl. Add enough boiling water to cover and set aside for 1–2 minutes. Remove the tomatoes from the water. Peel the skins from the tomatoes and chop the flesh. Set aside.
2 Heat the oil in a large frying pan over medium heat. Add the garlic and green shallots, and cook for 2 minutes or until the green shallots begin to soften.
3 Add the tomatoes, stock, bay leaf and sugar, and cook, uncovered, stirring often, for 5 minutes or until tomato begins to break down.
4 Place the fish fillets in the tomato sauce in a single layer, skin-side up. Cover with a lid or foil, reduce heat to medium-low and cook for 1–1½ minutes each side or until the fish is just cooked through and flakes when tested with a fork.
5 Transfer the fish to a plate and cover with foil to keep warm. Increase heat to high and simmer the sauce for 5 minutes or until it thickens slightly. Stir in the basil, then taste and season with salt and pepper.
6 Cut each fish fillet in half, place on serving plates and spoon the sauce over. Serve immediately with the crusty bread.

nutritional information per serving: 36g protein, 8g fat, 7g carbohydrate, 4g dietary fibre, 1,035kJ (245 Cals).

microwave instructions: follow step 1.
2 Place the oil, garlic and green shallots in a 6cm-deep, square, 25cm (base diameter) heatproof microwave-safe dish and cook, uncovered, on High/800watts/100% for 1 minute.
3 Add tomatoes, stock, bay leaf and sugar. Cook on High/800watts/100% for 3–4 minutes or until the tomatoes begin to break down.
4 Place the fish in the tomato sauce, cover loosely with damp paper towel and cook on Medium/500watts/50% for 10 minutes or until the fish is just cooked through and flakes when tested with a fork.
5 Transfer fish to a plate and cover to keep warm. Cook the sauce on High/800watts/100% for 3–5 minutes or until it thickens slightly. Stir in the basil and season with salt and pepper. Continue with step 6.

ROAST CHICKEN & VEGETABLES WITH LEMON CHILLI SAUCE & COUSCOUS

*You're on your own so take a risk—
try a fruity verdelho from Seaview or Tulloch*

JUST FOR ONE

I love eating alone—it means you can eat what you want. But if you have to share, this menu can be doubled easily and successfully.

ROAST CHICKEN & VEGETABLES WITH LEMON CHILLI SAUCE & COUSCOUS

serves: 1   prep: 15 mins   cooking: 20 mins

1	ripe egg tomato, quartered lengthways
1	small zucchini, halved, quartered lengthways
1 tbs	olive oil
	Salt & ground black pepper, to taste
½ tsp	ground cumin
1	single chicken breast fillet, fat trimmed
80ml	(⅓ cup) water or chicken stock
70g	(⅓ cup) couscous

lemon chilli sauce

1 tbs	fresh lemon juice
2 tsp	olive oil
½	fresh red chilli, deseeded, finely chopped
1 tbs	roughly chopped coriander leaves
	Salt & ground black pepper, to taste

1 Preheat oven to 250°C. Line a baking tray with non-stick baking paper.

2 Place the tomato and zucchini in a bowl. Add 2 tsp of oil, season with salt and pepper, and toss to coat. Place the vegetables, cut-side up, on the lined tray. Roast in preheated oven for 10 minutes.

3 Place 1 tsp of the remaining oil in a small bowl. Add the cumin, salt and pepper, and mix well. Add the chicken and turn to coat.

4 Place the chicken on the lined tray with the vegetables and roast in preheated oven for 5 minutes. Reduce oven temperature to 200°C and roast for a further 10 minutes or until chicken is just cooked through.

5 Meanwhile, to make the sauce, place the lemon juice, oil and chilli in a small bowl. Use a fork to whisk until well combined. Stir in the coriander and season with salt and pepper. Set aside.

6 Place the water or stock in a small saucepan and bring to the boil. (See microwave tip.) Remove from heat and add couscous while stirring with a fork. Cover and set aside for 2–3 minutes or until all the liquid is absorbed. Add remaining 1 tsp of oil and season with salt. Place over medium heat and stir with a fork for 1 minute or until warm.

7 Spoon the couscous onto a plate, top with the chicken and spoon the sauce over. Serve with the roasted vegetables.

microwave tip: place the water or stock in a medium, heatproof microwave-safe bowl.
Cover with a lid or plastic wrap and heat on High/800watts/100% for 1–2 minutes or until the liquid comes to the boil.

winter menu for four (for under $15)

AVOCADO WITH WARM MUSTARD DRESSING

TOMATO, PANCETTA & PARMESAN PASTA

For a fresh and lively sauvignon blanc—try the delicious Montana or Corbans from the Marlborough region in the South Island of New Zealand

BUDGET-FRIENDLY

I'm often on the lookout for recipes that are impressive yet inexpensive. I've found the key is using fresh produce when it's in season and simple flavour combinations. This menu delivers on all fronts.

AVOCADO WITH WARM MUSTARD DRESSING

serves: 4   prep: 10 mins   cooking: 2 mins

  1   lemon, rind finely grated, juiced
60ml   (¼ cup) extra virgin olive oil
  2   garlic cloves, crushed
1 tsp   wholegrain mustard
            Pinch of sugar
            Salt & ground black pepper, to taste
  2   ripe avocados, halved, stone removed, peeled
  1   bunch rocket, trimmed, washed, dried
35g   (¼ cup) walnut pieces, finely chopped

1   Combine ½ tsp of the lemon rind and 1½ tbs of the lemon juice with the oil, garlic, mustard and sugar in a small saucepan (reserve any remaining lemon rind and juice for another use). Heat over medium-low heat for 1–2 minutes or until the mixture is just warm. (See microwave tip.) Season well with salt and pepper, and whisk until well combined.

2   Cut each avocado half into 4 slices lengthways. Arrange the rocket leaves and avocado slices on serving plates and drizzle with the warm dressing. Sprinkle with walnuts and serve immediately.

microwave tip: combine ½ tsp of the lemon rind and 1½ tbs of the lemon juice with the oil, garlic, mustard and sugar in a small, heatproof microwave-safe bowl. Heat, uncovered, on High/800watts/100% for 1 minute or until just warm.

TOMATO, PANCETTA & PARMESAN PASTA

serves: 4   prep: 10 mins   cooking: 15 mins

  1 tbs   olive oil
    1   brown onion, finely diced
    2   garlic cloves, crushed
    1   small fresh red chilli, deseeded, thinly sliced
100g   (about 6 thin slices) pancetta, cut into thin strips
    1   400g can diced tomatoes
250ml   (1 cup) vegetable stock
60ml   (¼ cup) water
400g   dried macaroni pasta
            Salt & ground black pepper, to taste
60g   (¾ cup) finely shredded parmesan

1   Heat the oil in a large frying pan over medium heat. Add the onion, garlic, chilli and pancetta. Cook, stirring occasionally, for 3–4 minutes or until the onion softens slightly. (See microwave tip 1.)

2   Add the tomatoes, stock and water, and stir to combine. Bring to the boil over medium-high heat. Reduce heat and simmer, uncovered, for 10 minutes or until the sauce reduces slightly. (See microwave tip 2.)

3   Meanwhile, cook the pasta in a large saucepan of salted boiling water, following packet directions, until al dente. Drain and return to the pan.

4   Season the sauce well with salt and pepper. Add to the pasta with 40g (½ cup) of parmesan and toss to combine. Taste and adjust the seasoning if necessary. Serve sprinkled with the remaining parmesan.

microwave tip 1: place the oil, onion, garlic, chilli and pancetta in a 2-litre (8-cup), heatproof microwave-safe bowl. Cook, uncovered, on High/800watts/100%, stirring every minute, for 2 minutes or until the onion softens slightly.

microwave tip 2: add the tomatoes, stock and water, and stir to combine. Cook, uncovered, on High/800watts/100%, stirring every 2 minutes, for 5–6 minutes or until the sauce reduces slightly.

summer menu for four

CHILLI PORK &
ASIAN GREENS STIR-FRY

LYCHEES IN LEMON GRASS
& MINT SYRUP

*A fresh semillon–sauvignon blanc blend—
Four Sisters won't let you down and Cape Mentelle
from Western Australia should be a special treat*

ASIAN OCCASION

*When I'm in a hurry, stir-frying is my
saviour. Pull out your wok and let it
bring fresh Asian flavours to your table
in no time. Finish the meal with a
refreshing, tropical dessert.*

CHILLI PORK & ASIAN GREENS STIR-FRY

serves: 4 prep: 20 mins cooking: 10 mins

2 tbs soy sauce

1 tbs oyster sauce

2 garlic cloves, crushed

½ long fresh red chilli, finely chopped

500g pork fillet, fat trimmed, thinly sliced

500g hokkien noodles

1 bunch baby bok choy

1 bunch choy sum

2 tbs peanut oil

1 red capsicum, quartered, deseeded,
cut into 1cm-thick strips

1 Combine the soy sauce, oyster sauce, garlic and chilli in a medium glass or ceramic bowl. Add the pork and stir well to coat. Cover and place in the fridge for 10 minutes to marinate.

2 Meanwhile, place the noodles in a large heatproof bowl and add enough boiling water to cover. Set aside for 2 minutes to soften slightly. Drain, place in a large bowl, cover to keep warm and set aside.

3 Trim the bases of the bok choy and choy sum, separate the leaves and wash well. Cut in half to separate the leaves from the stems.

4 Heat a wok over high heat for 1–2 minutes or until hot. Add 2 tsp of oil and heat for 30 seconds. Add half the marinated pork and stir-fry for 1 minute or until just tender. Transfer to a plate and set aside. Repeat with another 2 tsp of oil and the remaining marinated pork.

5 Add the remaining 1 tbs of oil to the wok and heat for 30 seconds or until very hot. Add the capsicum and bok choy and choy sum stems, and stir-fry for 1 minute. Return the pork to the wok with the bok choy and choy sum leaves. Stir-fry for 1 minute or until the pork is heated through and the bok choy and choy sum leaves wilt.

6 Add the noodles and toss gently to combine. Serve immediately.

LYCHEES IN LEMON GRASS & MINT SYRUP

serves: 4 prep: 10 mins (+ 30 mins standing time) cooking: 10 mins

You can make the syrup up to 2 days before serving. Store in an airtight container in the fridge.

2 lemon grass stems, trimmed

500ml (2 cups) water

225g (1 cup) sugar

4 fresh mint sprigs

28 lychees, peeled

Vanilla ice-cream, to serve

1 Cut the lemon grass in half lengthways. Use the flat side of a large knife to flatten and bruise the lemon grass on a chopping board.

2 Place the lemon grass, water, sugar and mint in a medium saucepan. Stir over medium heat until the sugar dissolves. Increase heat to high and bring to the boil. Boil, uncovered, for 5 minutes. (See microwave tip.) Remove from the heat and set aside for 30 minutes to infuse and cool to room temperature. Discard the lemon grass and mint.

3 To serve, divide the lychees among serving bowls, spoon the syrup over and serve with ice-cream.

microwave tip: place the lemon grass, water, sugar and mint in a 1-litre (4-cup), heatproof microwave-safe bowl. Cook, uncovered, on High/800watts/100%, stirring every 2 minutes, for 6–8 minutes or until the sugar dissolves and the syrup thickens slightly.

RED WINE & ROSEMARY STEAKS
WITH CHAT POTATOES

MIXED SALAD LEAVES

---

*Simply requires a rich and soft shiraz
from the Barossa Valley in South Australia,
like Richmond Grove or Grant Burge*

FUSS-FREE & FOOLPROOF

When I cook this dish, I pour a glass of red for myself and some for the marinade (remember, it will only be as good as the wine you use).

RED WINE & ROSEMARY STEAKS WITH CHAT POTATOES

serves: 2   prep: 10 mins (+ 30 mins marinating time)   cooking: 25 mins

2   (180–200g each) beef scotch fillet
    (rib eye) steaks, fat trimmed

12   (about 540g) chat (small coliban) potatoes

10g   (2 tsp) butter, at room temperature
    Salt & ground black pepper, to taste
    Mixed salad leaves, washed, dried, to serve

red wine & rosemary marinade

60ml   (¼ cup) red wine

1 tbs   olive oil

1½ tsp   balsamic vinegar

3   green shallots, trimmed, chopped

1   large garlic clove, crushed

2 tsp   fresh rosemary leaves
    Salt & ground black pepper, to taste

1   To make the marinade, place the wine, oil, vinegar, green shallots, garlic, rosemary, salt and pepper in a blender. Blend until the green shallots and rosemary are finely chopped.

2   Place the steaks in a shallow glass or ceramic dish. Add the marinade and turn the steaks to coat. Cover and place in the fridge for 30 minutes to marinate.

3   Place the potatoes in a medium saucepan and cover with plenty of cold water. Cover and bring to the boil over high heat. Reduce heat to medium-high and cook, uncovered, for 15 minutes or until tender. Drain and return the potatoes to the pan. Add the butter, season with salt and pepper, and toss to coat.

4   Meanwhile, preheat barbecue grill or chargrill on medium-high. Cook the drained steaks on preheated grill, turning once and brushing with the marinade occasionally, for 4 minutes each side for medium or until cooked to your liking. Serve with the potatoes and salad leaves.

spring menu for four

SPRING VEGETABLE SOUP

CRUSTY BREAD

BROAD BEAN & GARLIC PASTA

A soft, plummy merlot from
Jamiesons Run or Preece

A VEGETABLE FEAST

This menu is incredibly simple, yet flavoursome, and perfectly suited to vegetarians. What better way to brush away the winter cobwebs than an abundance of spring vegetables?

SPRING VEGETABLE SOUP

serves: 4   prep: 15 mins   cooking: 30 mins

This soup can be made to the end of step 2 up to 2 days ahead. Reheat over medium heat—add the spinach and snow peas just before serving.

2 tbs olive oil
2 leeks, white part only, washed, thickly sliced
2 celery sticks, thinly sliced
1 coliban (washed) potato, peeled, diced
2 garlic cloves, finely chopped
1L (4 cups) vegetable stock
250ml (1 cup) water
3 fresh thyme sprigs
1 bunch English spinach, stems trimmed, washed
100g snow peas, ends trimmed, diagonally sliced
Salt & ground black pepper, to taste
Lemon wedges & crusty bread, to serve

1 Heat the oil in a large saucepan over medium heat. Add the leeks, celery, potato and garlic, and cook, uncovered, stirring often, for 8–10 minutes or until the leeks soften slightly.

2 Add the stock, water and thyme to the pan, and stir to combine. Cover, increase heat to high and bring to the boil. Reduce heat to medium and simmer, uncovered, for 10 minutes or until the potato is tender.

3 Roughly chop the spinach, then add to the soup with the snow peas. Simmer, uncovered, for a further 2 minutes or until the spinach wilts and the snow peas are bright green and tender crisp. Taste and season with salt and pepper.

4 Serve the soup with the lemon wedges and crusty bread.

BROAD BEAN & GARLIC PASTA

serves: 4   prep: 15 mins   cooking: 15 mins

You can use 1.6kg fresh broad beans in this recipe (this will make 450g when shelled). Remove from the pods and cook in boiling water for 3–4 minutes or until just tender and bright green. Drain, remove skins and continue from step 3.

350g dried pasta bows
450g (3 cups) frozen broad beans
60ml (¼ cup) extra virgin olive oil
1 brown onion, finely chopped
4 garlic cloves, thinly sliced
⅓ cup chopped fresh continental parsley
Salt & ground black pepper, to taste
Parmesan shavings, to serve

1 Cook the pasta in a large saucepan of salted boiling water, following packet directions, until al dente. Drain, return to the pan and cover to keep warm.

2 Meanwhile, cook the beans, following packet directions, until just tender. (See microwave tip.) Drain, remove the skins and set aside.

3 Heat the oil in a large, heavy-based frying pan over medium heat. Add the onion and garlic, and cook, stirring occasionally, for 5 minutes or until the onion softens slightly. Increase heat to high and add the beans. Cook, stirring, for 1–2 minutes or until heated through. Stir in the parsley.

4 Add the bean mixture to the pasta and toss to combine. Taste and season with salt and pepper. Serve sprinkled with parmesan shavings.

microwave tip: place the beans in a freezer bag with 1 tsp water and twist the opening to secure. Cook on High/800watts/100% for 2–3 minutes or until just tender.

summer menu for two

FISH BAKED IN PAPER WITH HERBED RICE

STRAWBERRY & PAPAYA SALAD

---

*I love young semillon from the Hunter Valley
in New South Wales with blue-eye trevalla—try any
from Tyrrell's or Brokenwood*

WHEAT &
DAIRY FREE

*Fabulous-tasting food doesn't have to involve
wheat- or dairy-based ingredients. This menu
is a great example.*

FISH BAKED IN PAPER WITH HERBED RICE

serves: 2   prep: 15 mins   cooking: 15 mins

2   (about 180g each) blue-eye trevalla
    cutlets or skinless fillets
65g (¼ cup) drained chargrilled
    capsicum strips
4   green shallots, white part only,
    cut into long strips
1 tbs dry white wine or fresh lemon juice
    Salt & ground black pepper, to taste
    Lemon wedges, to serve

herbed rice
100g (½ cup) long-grain white rice
1 tbs olive oil
250ml (1 cup) vegetable stock
2 tbs snipped fresh chives
2 tbs chopped fresh continental parsley leaves

1 Preheat oven to 200°C. Cut two 40cm-long pieces of non-stick baking paper.
2 To make the herbed rice, rinse the rice in a sieve under cold running water until water runs clear. Heat oil in a small heavy-based saucepan over medium heat. Add the rice and cook, stirring, for 1 minute.
3 Increase heat to high, add stock, cover and bring to the boil. Reduce heat to low and simmer gently for 12 minutes or until tender.
4 Meanwhile, place a fish cutlet or fillet in the centre of each piece of baking paper. Toss capsicum and green shallots together and arrange over fish. Drizzle with wine and sprinkle with a little salt and pepper.
5 Fold edges of paper together and tuck ends under to enclose the fish. Place on a baking tray and bake in preheated oven for 8–10 minutes or until the fish is just cooked and flakes when tested with a fork.
6 To serve, add chives and parsley to rice and use a fork to combine. Open the parcels and transfer the fish to serving plates. Drizzle with the cooking juices and serve with the herbed rice and lemon wedges.

nutritional information per serving: 49g protein, 12g fat, 42g carbohydrate, 2g dietary fibre, 1,990kJ (475 Cals).

STRAWBERRY & PAPAYA SALAD

serves: 2   prep: 10 mins (+ 10 mins standing time)

1   ripe small papaya, quartered, deseeded,
    peeled, cut into small wedges
250g (2 punnets) strawberries, washed,
    hulled, quartered
2   passionfruit, halved, pulp removed
2 tbs fresh orange juice
2 tsp honey

1 Place the papaya, strawberries, passionfruit pulp, orange juice and honey in a medium bowl and toss gently to combine.
2 Cover and set aside for 10 minutes to allow the flavours to develop before serving.

nutritional information per serving: 4g protein, 0g fat, 29g carbohydrate, 13g dietary fibre, 585kJ (140 Cals).

autumn menu for four

MUSHROOM, LEEK & SPINACH RISOTTO

ICE-CREAM WITH HOT FUDGE SAUCE

A classic dish deserves a classic partner—
try the ever-reliable Metala Shiraz Cabernet
or Koonunga Hill Shiraz Cabernet Sauvignon

FAST & FABULOUS

Risotto can be fast and fabulous (and will soon
be a favourite!) if cooked in the microwave.
This menu is also vegetarian-friendly—just
use vegetable stock instead of chicken stock.

MUSHROOM, LEEK & SPINACH RISOTTO

serves: 4   prep: 15 mins (+ 3 mins standing time)   cooking: 23 mins

2 tbs olive oil

2 leeks, trimmed, halved lengthways, washed, dried, thinly sliced

2 garlic cloves, crushed

440g (2 cups) arborio rice

1L (4 cups) chicken or vegetable stock

350g Swiss brown mushrooms, sliced

1 bunch English spinach, trimmed, washed, dried, shredded

2 tbs fresh thyme leaves

100g parmesan, grated

Ground black pepper, to taste

Parmesan shavings, to serve

1 Place the oil, leeks and garlic in a 3-litre (12-cup), heatproof microwave-safe bowl or microwave rice cooker. Cook, uncovered, on High/800watts/100%, stirring every minute, for 2 minutes. Stir in the rice. Cook, uncovered, on High/800watts/100% for 1 minute.

2 Stir in 750ml (3 cups) of the stock. Cover with a lid or double layer of plastic wrap and cook on High/800watts/100% for 5 minutes, followed by Medium/500watts/50% for 8 minutes.

3 Carefully remove the lid or plastic wrap. Working quickly to prevent too much steam escaping, stir in the mushrooms and remaining 250ml (1 cup) stock. Cover and cook, on Medium/500watts/50% for a further 7 minutes or until almost all the liquid is absorbed.

4 Stir in spinach and thyme. Cover with the lid or foil and set aside for 3 minutes or until spinach wilts. Stir in grated parmesan with a fork. Season with pepper and serve sprinkled with parmesan shavings.

ICE-CREAM WITH HOT FUDGE SAUCE

serves: 4   prep: 5 mins   cooking: 3 mins

This recipe makes about 300ml fudge sauce, which is a very generous amount for 4 people. However, it will keep for up to 2 weeks in an airtight jar in the fridge. The sauce is also delicious served warm over fresh strawberries, toasted waffles or pancakes.

185ml (³/₄ cup) sweetened condensed milk

50g (2½ tbs) butter, cubed

2 tbs golden syrup

150g good-quality dark chocolate, chopped

1½ tsp vanilla essence

Vanilla ice-cream, to serve

1 Place the condensed milk, butter and golden syrup in a 1-litre (4-cup) heatproof microwave-safe glass jug or bowl.

2 Cook, uncovered, on High/800watts/100%, whisking every 30 seconds, for 2–2½ minutes or until the mixture thickens and is light golden.

3 Remove from the microwave and place on a heatproof surface. Add the chocolate and vanilla essence, and use a wooden spoon to stir until the chocolate melts and the sauce is smooth.

4 To serve, scoop the ice-cream into serving glasses or bowls and top with 2–3 spoonfuls of the hot fudge sauce.

tip: to reheat the sauce, spoon the required amount into a heatproof microwave-safe jug or bowl. Heat, uncovered, on Medium-High/650watts/70%, stirring every minute, for 1–2 minutes or until melted and warm.

autumn menu for four

LEMON GRASS BEEF WITH NOODLES

CARDAMOM PEARS

*This is a definite beer menu, and James Boag's and
Cascade Pale Ale from Tasmania are as good as it gets*

A QUICK FIX

*Lemon grass, lime and cardamom are some of
my favourite flavours. They all make their
mark in this simple, quick and fresh menu.*

LEMON GRASS BEEF WITH NOODLES

serves: 4   prep: 10 mins   cooking: 10–12 mins

3	lemon grass stems, pale section only
600g	lean beef rump steaks, thinly sliced across the grain
80ml	(⅓ cup) peanut oil
6cm	piece fresh ginger, peeled, cut into matchsticks
3	garlic cloves, finely chopped
1	250g pkt rice vermicelli noodles
250g	green beans, topped, diagonally sliced
60ml	(¼ cup) fresh lime juice
250g	bean sprouts
1	bunch mint, leaves picked, shredded
1	bunch coriander, leaves picked
1 tbs	kecap manis (sweet Indonesian soy sauce)
	Salt & ground black pepper, to taste

1 Use the flat side of a knife to bruise the lemon grass stems and then finely chop. Combine with the beef, oil, ginger and garlic in a large bowl. Cover and set aside to marinate while cooking the noodles.

2 Cook the noodles in a large saucepan of boiling water for 3 minutes or until just tender. Drain and cover to keep warm.

3 Heat a large wok or non-stick frying pan over high heat until it is just smoking. Add a quarter of the beef mixture and stir-fry for 1 minute. Transfer to a bowl and repeat with remaining beef mixture in 3 batches. Add the beans and 1 tbs of lime juice, and stir-fry for 2 minutes or until the beans are bright green.

4 Return beef and any juices to the wok with the noodles, bean sprouts, mint, coriander, remaining lime juice, kecap manis, salt and pepper. Toss gently until combined and heated through. Serve immediately.

CARDAMOM PEARS

serves: 4   prep: 5 mins   cooking: 15–20 mins

375ml	(1½ cups) water
125g	(¾ cup, lightly packed) brown sugar
½ tsp	ground cardamom
4	just-ripe pears (like williams), peeled, quartered, cored
	Natural yoghurt or thickened cream, to serve

1 Place the water, sugar and cardamom in a large saucepan. Stir over medium heat until the sugar dissolves.

2 Add the pears to the syrup and bring to a simmer. Simmer, uncovered, turning the pears occasionally, for 10–15 minutes or until they are just tender. (See microwave tip.) Serve warm or at room temperature with the yoghurt or cream.

microwave tip: place the water, sugar and cardamom in a 6cm-deep, square, 25cm heatproof microwave-safe dish. Cook on High/800watts/100%, stirring every minute, for 2–3 minutes or until the sugar dissolves. Add the pears to the syrup and cook on High/800watts/100%, turning the pears halfway through cooking, for 8–10 minutes or until they are just tender.

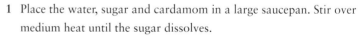

LONG
LUNCHES

Lengthy, uncomplicated and lazy is the way I think all lunches should be. Take time to relish good food and good wine. Move to the backyard to savour smoky barbecue flavours, or pack a portable feast and make the great outdoors your dining room. Warm your home and fill the air with the comforting aromas that waft out of slow-cooked dishes, then relax with a long bottle of red.

These menus are designed to stretch into the late afternoon, leaving everyone, including the cook, feeling relaxed and content.

HALOUMI SALAD
WITH BALSAMIC DRESSING

BARLEY, SPLIT PEA &
PUMPKIN PILAF

EGGPLANT WITH YOGHURT
& MINT DRESSING

ORANGE & LEMON GRANITA

McWilliams Riverina Tyrian is a new and exciting red wine made from a variety specially bred for Australia—give it a try, it's delicious. Another unique Aussie wine that suits this menu perfectly is Brown Brothers Tarrango

MEDITERRANEAN-STYLE VEGETARIAN

The people of the Mediterranean are certainly familiar with long, languid lunches—they're a perfected pastime in that part of the world. The region encompasses many countries, all with their own typical flavours. This menu acts as a mixing pot, combining elements of them all to create something wonderful and balanced. The flavours are comforting yet refreshing, earthy yet light. A perfect lunch.

HALOUMI SALAD WITH BALSAMIC DRESSING

picture page 31

serves: 6   prep: 20–25 mins   cooking: 2–4 mins

2   Lebanese cucumbers
150g   baby spinach leaves, rinsed, dried
4   vine-ripened tomatoes, halved,
      cut into 1cm-thick slices
1   bunch mint, washed, dried, leaves picked
80ml   (⅓ cup) extra virgin olive oil
60ml   (¼ cup) balsamic vinegar
2   250g pkts haloumi, drained
50g   (⅓ cup) plain flour, for dusting
      Salt & ground black pepper, to taste

1   Run a vegetable peeler down the length of the cucumbers to form ribbons. Toss together with the spinach, tomatoes and mint.

2   Pour 60ml (¼ cup) of the oil and the vinegar into a small jug. Use a fork to whisk until well combined and the dressing begins to thicken. Set aside.

3   Cut each piece of haloumi into 3 slices, then cut each slice in half to form triangles. Place the flour on a plate and toss the haloumi in the flour to lightly coat. Shake off any excess.

4   Heat the remaining 1 tbs oil in a large non-stick frying pan over medium-high heat. Cook half the haloumi slices for 30–60 seconds each side or until light golden and warmed through. Transfer to a plate and set aside. Repeat with the remaining haloumi slices.

5   Divide the spinach mixture among serving plates. Place the haloumi on top and drizzle with the balsamic dressing. Sprinkle with salt and pepper, and serve immediately.

BARLEY, SPLIT PEA & PUMPKIN PILAF

serves: 6   prep: 20 mins   cooking: 1 hour

30g   (1½ tbs) butter
1 tbs   olive oil
2   brown onions, thinly sliced
3   garlic cloves, finely chopped
3 tsp   cumin seeds
105g   (½ cup) pearl barley
110g   (½ cup) dried yellow split peas
875ml   (3½ cups) chicken stock
2kg   butternut pumpkin, peeled, deseeded,
      cut into 2cm chunks
      Salt & ground black pepper, to taste
½ cup   fresh coriander leaves
      Lebanese bread, to serve

1   Heat the butter and oil in a large saucepan over medium heat. Add the onions, garlic and cumin seeds, and cook, stirring occasionally, for 5–6 minutes or until the onions begin to soften and the mixture is aromatic.

2   Add the barley and split peas, and cook, stirring often, for 3 minutes or until well coated in the onion mixture.

3   Stir in the stock, increase heat to high and bring to the boil. Reduce heat to low, cover and cook gently for 30 minutes.

4   Add the pumpkin to the pan and stir well. Cover, increase heat to high and return to the boil. Reduce heat to low and cook for a further 10–12 minutes or until pumpkin is tender and almost all the liquid is absorbed. Remove from heat and season with salt and pepper.

5   Serve immediately or set aside, uncovered, for 30 minutes or until cooled to room temperature. Use a fork to stir in the coriander just before serving with the Lebanese bread.

EGGPLANT WITH YOGHURT & MINT DRESSING

picture page 32

serves: 6   prep: 5 mins   cooking: 12 mins

80g   (½ cup) pine nuts

9   (about 650g) baby eggplant,
     halved lengthways

60ml   (¼ cup) olive oil

yoghurt & mint dressing

180g   (⅔ cup) Greek-style natural yoghurt

2 tsp   honey

2 tbs   shredded fresh mint leaves
        Salt & ground black pepper, to taste

1   Place the pine nuts in a large non-stick frying pan over medium heat and cook, stirring often, for 3–4 minutes or until golden. Set aside.

2   To make dressing, place yoghurt, honey and mint in a medium bowl. Use a fork to whisk until well combined. Season with salt and pepper.

3   Place the eggplant and oil in a large bowl and toss to coat. Heat a large chargrill or the non-stick frying pan over high heat. Add half the eggplant, reduce heat to medium-high and cook for 3–4 minutes each side or until tender. Transfer the eggplant to a serving plate or bowl, cover loosely with foil and set aside. Repeat with remaining eggplant.

4   To serve, drizzle the eggplant with the dressing and sprinkle with the toasted pine nuts. Serve warm or at room temperature.

ORANGE & LEMON GRANITA

serves: 6   prep: 15 mins (+ 1 hour chilling and 11 hours freezing time)

225g   (1 cup) sugar

375ml   (1½ cups) boiling water

250ml   (1 cup) fresh lemon juice, strained

250ml   (1 cup) fresh orange juice, strained

1 tbs   finely grated orange rind

1   Place the sugar in a medium heatproof bowl. Add the boiling water and stir until the sugar dissolves. Cover and place in the fridge for 1 hour or until chilled.

2   Place the chilled syrup, lemon juice, orange juice and orange rind in a 2-litre (8-cup) non-aluminium container and stir to combine. Cover with a lid or foil and freeze for 3 hours or until partially frozen.

3   Use a fork to break the frozen portions of the granita into large chunks, then draw them into the centre. Cover and return to the freezer for 8 hours or overnight to set completely.

4   Use a sturdy fork to scrape the granita into coarse crystals. Cover and return to the freezer until required.

5   Spoon granita into chilled glasses or bowls and serve immediately.

SMOKED SALMON BAGUETTE

LEMON & ROSEMARY
MARINATED VEAL SKEWERS

SEASONAL FRUIT

COCONUT BISCUITS

LIME & GINGER CORDIAL

*Traditional red styles like Houghton's Cabernet
Shiraz Merlot or Tatachilla's Partners Cabernet
Sauvignon Shiraz are lovely, a bit
spicy and soft—perfecto*

THE PERFECT PICNIC

*The family picnics I grew up with in country
New South Wales were simple affairs enjoyed
after a long muster on horseback. Mum would
meet us by the creek and we would cook thin
beef sausages over an open fire made from old
eucalyptus branches. This menu is more
sophisticated, but still with an emphasis on ease
and simplicity—for a special, but relaxed day
with friends.*

SMOKED SALMON BAGUETTE

picture page 37

serves: 6   prep: 15 mins (+ 10 mins cooling time)   cooking: 10 mins

The zucchini can be cooked up to 4 hours before going on your picnic, and the baguette can be assembled up to 2 hours before.
For a variation, try combining ingredients like marinated vegetables, deli meats, cheese, pesto and salad greens.

2   40cm baguettes (French sticks)

2   large (about 120g each) zucchini, ends trimmed, thinly sliced lengthways

180g   (1 cup) semi-dried tomatoes

85g   (⅓ cup) bought olive tapenade

1   large bunch (about 160g) rocket, stems trimmed, leaves washed, dried

16   large fresh basil leaves

200g   (about 10 slices) smoked salmon

1   Use a serrated knife to make a lengthways cut into the top of each baguette (don't cut all the way through). Use your fingers to remove the soft bread from the centre of each, leaving a 1cm-thick shell. (Reserve the bread to make breadcrumbs for another use.)

2   Preheat a chargrill or non-stick frying pan over high heat. Cook the zucchini on preheated chargrill or in pan for 2 minutes each side or until just tender.

3   Place the semi-dried tomatoes and olive tapenade in a small bowl and mix well. Line the inside of the baguettes with rocket leaves, letting some hang over the top. Spread the semi-dried tomato mixture over the bottom of the baguettes. Top with the zucchini slices and use your fingers to press firmly into place. Top with the basil leaves and then the salmon, letting some salmon hang over the top.

4   Use your hands to close the baguettes and press firmly to allow the filling to settle. Holding the baguette firmly in one hand, carefully cut into 3 portions. Wrap each portion in waxed paper or plastic wrap and place in an airtight container in the fridge until ready to take on your picnic. Pack them close to ice bricks to keep them cool.

LEMON & ROSEMARY MARINATED VEAL SKEWERS

serves: 6   prep: 10 mins (+ 30 mins marinating time)   cooking: 5–7 mins

The veal can be marinated and cooked up to 1 hour before going on your picnic.

750g   (about 6) veal leg steaks, cut into 2cm-wide strips

lemon & rosemary marinade

2   lemons, rind finely grated, juiced

⅓ cup   fresh rosemary leaves

2 tbs   olive oil

1 tbs   ground cumin

4   garlic cloves, crushed
Salt & ground black pepper, to serve

1   Soak 18 bamboo skewers in water to prevent them sticking. To make marinade, place lemon rind and juice, rosemary, oil, cumin, garlic, salt and pepper in a medium glass or ceramic bowl. Add veal and toss to coat. Cover and place in the fridge for 30 minutes to marinate.

2   Preheat a chargrill, barbecue or frying pan over high heat. Thread 2–3 strips of veal onto each skewer. Cook a third of the skewers on preheated chargrill, turning occasionally, for 4–6 minutes or until just cooked. Set aside, uncovered. Repeat with the remaining skewers.

3   Allow the veal skewers to cool to room temperature, then place in an airtight container. Keep in the fridge until ready to take on your picnic. Pack the container close to ice bricks to keep them cool.

SEASONAL FRUIT

Fruit that is easy to eat and travels well is best for a picnic. Try pears (like packham, beurre bosc or williams), apples (like jonathan, golden delicious, fuji, granny smith or bonza), figs, grapes, guava, mandarins, nashi, plums and rambutans.

PICNIC TIPS

A small cooler bag or box, and ice bricks are essential if the weather is warm or if your picnic site is not nearby. Pack food and drinks close to the ice bricks to ensure they are chilled, fresh and ready to enjoy when you arrive. The only essential extras you'll need for this picnic are glasses for the drinks, a couple of napkins and perhaps a knife to cut the fruit. It is also a good idea to take a waterproof groundsheet to place under your picnic rug if you think the ground may be damp.

COCONUT BISCUITS

makes: about 18   prep: 15 mins   cooking: 15 mins

These biscuits will keep in an airtight container for up to 1 week.

2   egg whites, at room temperature
80g (⅓ cup) caster sugar
130g (1½ cups) desiccated coconut
1 tsp vanilla essence

1 Preheat oven to 170°C. Line 2 baking trays with non-stick baking paper.

2 Use electric beaters or a balloon whisk to whisk the egg whites in a clean, dry medium bowl until soft peaks form.

3 Gradually add the sugar, a spoonful at a time, whisking until the sugar dissolves and the mixture is thick and glossy. Add the coconut and vanilla essence, and use a large metal spoon or spatula to fold in until just combined.

4 Drop tablespoonsful of mixture separately onto the lined trays. Bake in preheated oven, swapping the trays halfway through cooking, for 15 minutes or until the biscuits are light golden and firm to the touch. Use the baking paper to lift the biscuits onto a wire rack to cool (they will firm slightly as they cool).

LIME & GINGER CORDIAL

makes: 400ml cordial base (enough for about 12 drinks)   prep: 10 mins

The cordial base will keep for up to 1 week in the fridge. Keep the cordial chilled while on your picnic.
Try adding a few drops of Angostura bitters to the finished cordial base for a slightly different flavour.

300ml fresh lime juice (10–12 limes)
220g (1 cup) caster sugar
5cm piece fresh ginger, peeled, roughly chopped
        Chilled water, sparkling mineral water, soda water or dry ginger ale, to serve
        Lime slices (optional), to serve

1 Place the lime juice, sugar and ginger in a blender, and blend until the sugar dissolves and the ginger is finely chopped.

2 Pour the mixture through a fine sieve into a bowl or jug, pressing firmly with the back of a spoon to remove any excess liquid from the pulp. Discard the pulp and transfer the juice to a clean bottle. Keep in the fridge until ready to mix or take on your picnic.

3 To mix, pour about 30ml (1½ tbs) of the cordial base into a glass and top with about 250ml (1 cup) chilled water, mineral water, soda water or dry ginger ale. Add a few lime slices before serving, if using.

winter menu for four

CAULIFLOWER SOUP

LAMB POT ROAST WITH
MUSHROOMS & ROSEMARY

CRUSTY BREAD

OAKLEAF SALAD WITH WALNUT DRESSING

CARAMEL ROASTED PEARS

*A lamb pot roast deserves a rich, cassis-dominant
wine like Leasingham Bin 56 Cabernet Malbec
or Annie's Lane Cabernet Merlot—both
from the Clare Valley in South Australia*

COSY &
COMFORTING

*I love recipes like these. Friendly, simple and
inviting, they are what you could call low
maintenance—after a little upfront work, they
make no more demands on your time. And the
results are wonderful—they will warm your
kitchen and comfort the soul during cool winter
days. This menu is perfect for a small gathering
with a long lunch in mind.*

CAULIFLOWER SOUP

picture page 43

serves: 4   prep: 15 mins (+ 5 mins cooling time)   cooking: 30 mins

40g	(2 tbs) butter
1	brown onion, chopped
1 tsp	ground or freshly grated nutmeg
1	medium (about 1.2kg) cauliflower, cut into florets
750ml	(3 cups) chicken or vegetable stock
250ml	(1 cup) water
	Salt & ground black pepper, to taste
	Thickened cream, to serve

1 Melt the butter in a large saucepan over medium heat. Add the onion and cook, stirring often, for 5 minutes or until soft. Add the nutmeg and cook, stirring, for 1 minute or until aromatic.

2 Stir in the cauliflower, stock and water. Increase heat to high, cover and bring to the boil. Reduce heat to medium-low and simmer, partially covered, for 20 minutes or until the cauliflower is very tender. Remove from heat and set aside for 5 minutes to cool slightly.

3 Place half the soup in a food processor and process until smooth. Return to a clean pan. Repeat with the remaining soup.

4 Reheat the soup over medium heat. Season well with salt and pepper. Serve garnished with cream and sprinkled with a little pepper.

LAMB POT ROAST WITH MUSHROOMS & ROSEMARY

serves: 4   prep: 15 mins   cooking: 2 hours 30–50 mins

1	(about 1.6kg) lamb forequarter rolled roast
3	garlic cloves, cut into thin slivers
	Salt & ground black pepper, to taste
50g	(2½ tbs) butter
2	red onions, halved, sliced
1	carrot, peeled, diced
1	celery stick, diced
3	sprigs fresh rosemary
3	sprigs fresh thyme
250g	large mushroom flats, sliced
125ml	(½ cup) dry red wine
	Crusty bread, to serve

1 Use a small sharp knife to make small incisions in the lamb and insert the garlic slivers. Rub the lamb all over with salt and pepper. Heat 20g (1 tbs) of butter in a large heavy-based saucepan or flameproof casserole dish over medium-high heat. Add the onions, carrot, celery, rosemary and thyme. Cover and cook, stirring occasionally, for 8–10 minutes or until the vegetables soften. Remove from the heat.

2 Meanwhile, heat 10g (2 tsp) of the remaining butter in a large heavy-based frying pan over high heat. Add the mushrooms and cook, stirring occasionally, for 3–5 minutes or until they are soft and lightly browned. Transfer to a bowl and set aside.

3 Melt the remaining 20g (1 tbs) of butter in the frying pan over high heat. Add the lamb and cook, turning occasionally, for 8–10 minutes or until well browned. (It is easiest to use 2 pairs of tongs to turn the lamb.) Place the lamb on top of the vegetables in the saucepan.

4 Add the wine to the frying pan and bring to the boil over high heat. Boil, scraping the pan with a wooden spoon to dislodge any cooked-on bits, for 1 minute. Pour the wine mixture over the lamb. Cover the pan and bring to the boil over high heat. Reduce heat to low (move the pan to a smaller hotplate if possible) and cook, turning the lamb 2–3 times during cooking, for 1½ hours. (As you turn the lamb, also check the level of liquid in the pan—if the lamb or vegetables are beginning to stick, add a little water, but only enough to prevent sticking—about 3–4 tbs.)

5 Add the cooked mushrooms to the pan, cover and cook, turning the lamb once, for a further 30 minutes or until the lamb is very tender and is easily pierced with a carving fork.

6 Transfer the lamb to a large plate and cover loosely with foil to keep warm. Remove the rosemary and thyme stems from the sauce. Return the pan to high heat and boil, uncovered, stirring occasionally, for 10–20 minutes or until the sauce reduces and thickens to a medium sauce consistency. Use a large shallow spoon to skim any excess fat from the surface of the sauce.

7 Carve the lamb and serve with the vegetables, sauce and bread.

OAKLEAF SALAD WITH WALNUT DRESSING

serves: 4   prep: 10 mins (+ 30 mins cooling time)   cooking: 5 mins

Oakleaf lettuce has fairly soft leaves with a wonderful mild, sweet flavour—
a world away from the well-known iceberg lettuce. It comes in red and green varieties,
both of which are suitable for this recipe.

2 tbs   olive oil

135g   (1⅓ cups) good-quality walnut halves

1 tbs   red wine vinegar

Salt & ground black pepper, to taste

1   oakleaf lettuce, leaves separated, washed, dried

1   Heat oil in a non-stick frying pan over medium heat. Cook walnuts, stirring often, for 5 minutes or until light golden. Use a slotted spoon to transfer half the walnuts to a small heatproof bowl and reserve.

2   Leave the remaining walnuts in the oil for 30 minutes or until cool. (See microwave tip.) Strain into a small jug or bowl (discard walnuts).

3   Add vinegar to oil and whisk well. Season with salt and pepper.

4   Toss dressing with lettuce in a bowl. Sprinkle with reserved walnuts.

microwave tip: place the walnuts in an oven bag and twist the opening to secure. Cook on High/800watts/100%, gently shaking the bag every minute, for 4–5 minutes or until light golden. Transfer half the walnuts to a heatproof bowl, add the oil and heat, uncovered, on High/800watts/100% for 2 minutes. Set aside for 30 minutes or until cool.

CARAMEL ROASTED PEARS

serves: 4   prep: 10 mins   cooking: 25–30 mins

These pears are heavenly. Their attraction lies not only in the divine
caramel sauce they bathe in, but in their simplicity—you only need five ingredients!
You can also serve them at room temperature.

4   just-ripe beurre bosc pears

30g   (1½ tbs) butter, melted

70g   (⅓ cup, firmly packed) brown sugar

80ml   (⅓ cup) thin cream

Double cream or vanilla ice-cream, to serve

1   Preheat oven to 200°C. Use an apple corer to remove the cores from the base of the pears, leaving the stems intact. Peel.

2   Stand the pears upright in a small ovenproof dish. Drizzle with the melted butter and sprinkle with the sugar. Bake in preheated oven for 10 minutes.

3   Pour the thin cream evenly over the pears and stir into the sugar mixture. Turn the pears to coat in the sauce and leave them lying on their sides. Bake, turning and brushing the pears occasionally, for a further 15–20 minutes or until they are tender when tested with a skewer. Serve warm with the double cream or ice-cream.

variation: CARAMEL BANANAS

Replace the pears with 4 just-ripe bananas, peeled and halved lengthways. After the cream is added, bake for a further 15 minutes. Serve warm, sprinkled with grated good-quality dark chocolate, if desired, and topped with a generous scoop of vanilla ice-cream.

spring menu for ten

PRAWN, ASPARAGUS & DILL SALAD

OCEAN TROUT WITH ROCKET, PARSLEY & TOMATO SALAD

CRUSTY BREAD

MANGO & COCONUT ICE WITH LIME MANGO

A little touch of herbaceousness and some fresh lemon characters make semillon–sauvignon blanc–chardonnay blends like Brokenwood's Cricket Pitch or Wirra Wirra's Scrubby Rise a perfect match

FROM THE SEA

Seafood, citrus and herbs have always had a blissful marriage. This fresh spring menu celebrates this partnership and brings to the table a simple seafood spread to linger over. When buying seafood, choose the freshest available and use as soon as possible to ensure full-flavoured dishes. The mango and coconut in the dessert are delicious proof that tropical flavours belong in a seafood menu.

PRAWN, ASPARAGUS & DILL SALAD

picture page 49

serves: 10   prep: 15 mins   cooking: 5 mins

Spring really is the best time to use asparagus in your cooking.
You will find slim, tender stems at a reasonable price without much trouble—
the best kind for a salad like this.

2   bunches fresh asparagus, ends trimmed, halved

2   Lebanese cucumbers

1.25kg   (about 30) cooked medium king prawns

dill dressing

125ml   (½ cup) olive oil

½ cup   chopped fresh dill leaves

80ml   (⅓ cup) fresh lemon juice

2 tsp   wholegrain mustard

Salt & ground black pepper, to taste

1 To make the dressing, place the oil, dill, lemon juice, mustard, salt and pepper in a small screw-top jar and shake well to combine. Set aside.

2 Cook asparagus in a saucepan of boiling water for 1–2 minutes or until bright green and just tender. (See microwave tip.) Drain and refresh under cold running water. Drain and place in a large bowl.

3 Run a vegetable peeler down the length of the cucumbers to form long ribbons. Peel and devein the prawns.

4 Add the prawns, cucumber and dill dressing to the asparagus, and toss to combine. Serve immediately.

microwave tip: wash asparagus, place in a freezer bag and twist the opening to secure. Cook on High/800watts/100% for 2–2½ minutes or until bright green and just tender.

OCEAN TROUT WITH ROCKET, PARSLEY & TOMATO SALAD

serves: 10   prep: 20 mins   cooking: 12–15 mins

The heat of the pan and the salt that you rub into the skin of the trout will make it nice and crisp—
a little trick to impress your guests. You can prepare the vegetables and herbs for the salad up to 6 hours ahead—
keep them in separate airtight containers in the fridge.

10   (about 180g each) ocean trout fillets

Olive oil, for brushing

Salt & ground black pepper, to taste

Crusty bread, to serve

rocket, parsley & tomato salad

500g   (2 punnets) cherry tomatoes, quartered

½ tsp   sugar

Salt & ground black pepper, to taste

2   bunches rocket, stems trimmed, washed, dried, roughly chopped

2   bunches continental parsley, washed, dried, leaves picked, roughly chopped

1   bunch green shallots, trimmed, sliced

80ml   (⅓ cup) olive or canola oil

60ml   (¼ cup) red wine vinegar

1 To make the salad, place the tomatoes in a large bowl, sprinkle with the sugar and ½ tsp salt, and toss to combine. Add the rocket, parsley, green shallots, oil, vinegar and pepper, and toss well to combine. Set aside.

2 Place a large non-stick frying pan over medium-high heat. Brush both sides of the trout fillets with the oil and rub the skin well with salt and pepper. Reduce heat to medium and add half the trout fillets, skin-side down, to the pan. Cook for 3 minutes each side for medium or until cooked to your liking. Transfer the cooked fillets to a plate, cover with foil to keep warm and set aside. Repeat with the remaining trout fillets.

3 Spoon the salad onto serving plates and place the trout fillets on top. Serve with the crusty bread.

MANGO & COCONUT ICE WITH LIME MANGO

serves: 10   prep: 25 mins (+ 15 mins cooling, 9–10 hours freezing and 1½ hours thawing time)   cooking: 1 min

You will need about 4 medium mangoes to make the mango & coconut ice. It will keep for up to 1 month.

2   400ml cans light coconut milk
220g   (1 cup) caster sugar
800g   chopped ripe mango flesh
2   egg whites

lime mango
2   limes
2 tbs   caster sugar
4   ripe medium mangoes

1   Combine the coconut milk and sugar in a medium saucepan. Stir over low heat for 1 minute or until sugar dissolves. (See microwave tip.) Remove from heat and set aside for 15 minutes or until lukewarm.

2   Place the mango flesh in the bowl of a food processor and process until smooth. Add to the cooled coconut milk mixture and mix until combined. Pour into a 2-litre (8-cup) freezer-proof container, cover and freeze for 3–4 hours or until lightly frozen.

3   Use electric beaters to whisk the egg whites in a clean, dry medium bowl until firm peaks form. Roughly break up the frozen mango mixture with a metal spoon and transfer to a large mixing bowl. Beat with the electric beaters until smooth. Use a large metal spoon to fold the egg whites into the mango mixture until well combined.

4   Return the mango mixture to the container and freeze for 6 hours or until frozen.

5   To make the lime mango, use a vegetable peeler to peel the rind from the limes. Remove the white pith and cut the rind into very thin strips. (Alternatively, use a zester.) Juice the limes. Combine the rind strips, lime juice and sugar in a medium bowl. Cut the cheeks from the mangoes close to the seeds and peel away the skin. Remove any remaining flesh from the seeds. Cut all the flesh lengthways into 1cm-thick slices. Add the mango slices to the lime mixture and mix gently to combine. Cover and place in the fridge until required.

6   Transfer the mango ice to the fridge 1–1½ hours before serving to soften slightly. Serve scoops of the ice with the lime mango.

microwave tip: combine the coconut milk and sugar in a medium microwave-safe jug or bowl. Heat, uncovered, on High/800watts/100% for 3 minutes. Stir well to dissolve the sugar.

autumn menu for eight

GOAT'S CHEESE SOUFFLES

WITLOF SALAD

NAVARIN OF LAMB

CRUSTY FRENCH BREAD

CRISP APPLE TART

Try a cooler-climate cabernet sauvignon from the Riverina and Central West regions in New South Wales —two notable producers are McWilliams Barwang and Rosemount Hill of Gold

FLAVOURS OF FRANCE

Creamy goat's cheese (also called chevre*), aromatic thyme, bitter witlof, tender lamb, crisp beans, dry white wine, buttery puff pastry and sweet apples are familiar ingredients on the French table, and are all readily available in Australia as well. This menu is about bringing French flavours into your home.*

The soufflés can be made completely and kept in the fridge for up to 2 hours before baking. Cook for 5 minutes longer if you do this.

GOAT'S CHEESE SOUFFLES

picture page 55

serves: 8   prep: 15 mins (+ 10 mins cooling time)   cooking: 35 mins

Melted butter, for greasing

Cornmeal (polenta), for coating

80g butter

75g (½ cup) plain flour

500ml (2 cups) milk

150g soft goat's cheese, crumbled

1 tsp finely chopped fresh thyme leaves

4 egg yolks

Salt & ground black pepper, to taste

6 egg whites, at room temperature

1 Preheat oven to 180°C. Brush eight 150ml soufflé dishes with melted butter to grease. Coat the inside of the dishes with cornmeal and shake out any excess. Place in a large ovenproof dish or roasting pan.

2 Melt the butter in a medium saucepan over medium heat. Add the flour and use a wooden spoon to stir until the mixture is smooth and beginning to bubble. Cook for 1 minute, stirring often. Remove from the heat and gradually add the milk, stirring until smooth and combined. Return to medium heat and stir until the mixture thickens and boils. Boil for 2 minutes, stirring constantly.

3 Remove from heat and stir in the goat's cheese and thyme. Spoon the mixture into a large bowl and set aside for 10 minutes to cool.

4 Add the egg yolks to the goat's cheese mixture and stir well to combine. Season with salt and pepper.

5 Use electric beaters or a balloon whisk to whisk the egg whites in a clean, dry large bowl until firm peaks form. Fold a large spoonful of egg whites into the goat's cheese mixture until well combined. Gently fold in the remaining egg whites until just combined.

6 Spoon mixture evenly into prepared dishes. Add enough boiling water to ovenproof dish or roasting pan to reach halfway up the sides of the soufflé dishes. Bake in preheated oven for 25 minutes or until puffed and golden. Serve immediately.

variation: TWICE-BAKED GOAT'S CHEESE SOUFFLES

Remove cooked soufflés from oven and set aside for 10 minutes to cool slightly. Turn the soufflés into a shallow ovenproof dish or individual dishes and set aside to cool to room temperature. Cover and refrigerate for up to 2 days or until required. Preheat oven to 180°C.

Pour 250ml (1 cup) thin cream evenly over the soufflés and then sprinkle with 40g (½ cup) finely grated parmesan.

Bake in preheated oven for 10–15 minutes or until light golden, warmed through and the cream is bubbling. Serve immediately.

NAVARIN OF LAMB

serves: 8   prep: 25 mins   cooking: 1½–2 hours

2kg (about 2) boned lamb shoulders

1 tbs olive oil

30g (1½ tbs) butter

1½ tbs plain flour

125ml (½ cup) dry white wine

750ml (3 cups) chicken stock

1 tbs tomato paste

3 garlic cloves, peeled, lightly crushed

1 large fresh rosemary sprig, cut into 8cm lengths

16 (about 600g) chat (small coliban) potatoes, halved

2 bunches spring onions

1 bunch baby carrots, trimmed, halved lengthways

300g green beans, topped

¼ cup fresh continental parsley leaves

Crusty French bread, to serve

1 Trim the lamb of any excess fat and cut into 2–3cm pieces.

2 Heat the oil and 20g (1 tbs) of the butter in a large heavy-based saucepan over high heat. Add a third of the lamb and cook, stirring occasionally, for 2–3 minutes or until well browned. Transfer to a bowl and set aside. Cook the remaining lamb in 2 more batches (add a little of the remaining butter to prevent sticking, if necessary).

3 Reduce heat to medium and melt any remaining butter in the pan. Add the flour and cook, stirring, for 2 minutes. Remove from the heat and gradually stir in the wine until smooth. Stir in the lamb, stock, tomato paste, garlic and rosemary. Return to high heat and bring to a simmer.

4 Reduce heat to low and simmer, covered, stirring occasionally, for 1 hour. Stir in the potatoes and cook, covered, for 20 minutes. Uncover and cook for a further 10 minutes or until the lamb is very tender and the potatoes are cooked.

5 Meanwhile, trim stems of spring onions about 5cm from the bulb and discard the tops. Remove the outer layer. Bring a large saucepan of water to the boil. Cook spring onion bulbs for 5 minutes or until just tender. Remove from pan with a slotted spoon, refresh under cold running water and set aside. Return water to the boil and repeat with carrots, cooking for 4–5 minutes or until just tender. Repeat with the beans, cooking for 1–2 minutes or until bright green and tender crisp.

6 Add the onions, carrots and beans to the lamb mixture, and stir well. Simmer for a further 4–5 minutes or until the vegetables are heated through. Stir in the parsley and serve with the crusty French bread.

WITLOF SALAD

picture page 55

serves: 8   prep: 5 mins

Witlof, also known as Belgian endive, has a pleasantly bitter flavour and crunchy texture—a perfect accompaniment to the delicate goat's cheese soufflés. It becomes bitter if exposed to too much light, so is best kept in a paper bag in the crisper section of the fridge and used within 2 days.

1 tbs   fresh lemon juice
½ tbs   olive oil
      Salt & ground black pepper, to taste
3   witlof, outer leaves discarded, inner leaves separated, washed, dried

1   Place the lemon juice, olive oil, salt and pepper in a small screw-top jar and shake well to combine.
2   Place the witlof leaves in a medium bowl, add the dressing and toss well to coat. Serve immediately.

CRISP APPLE TART

serves: 8   prep: 15 mins   cooking: 25 mins

2   sheets (25 x 25cm) ready-rolled frozen puff pastry
2   medium (about 150g each) golden delicious apples
20g   (1 tbs) butter, diced
1½ tbs   sugar
1 tbs   orange marmalade, warmed, sieved
      Double cream, to serve

1   Preheat oven to 200°C. Line 2 baking trays with non-stick baking paper.

2   Place a pastry sheet on each lined tray and cut a 2cm border around each sheet, only cutting halfway through.
3   Halve and core the apples. Place on a chopping board, cut-side down, and thinly slice widthways.
4   Place the apple slices in 3 rows down the centre of each pastry sheet. Dot with the butter and sprinkle with the sugar.
5   Bake in preheated oven for 25 minutes or until the pastry is crisp and golden. Gently brush the warmed marmalade over the apples and pastry border. Serve warm with the cream.

BEST ON THE BARBECUE

Barbecuing must be one of the simplest, most hassle-free ways of cooking, and I love it! This whole menu is dead easy (especially the cake, based on my Aunt Joey's recipe), making for an extra-relaxed lunch.

These dishes are also great to take on a barbecue picnic. Just make sure all the food is stored in well-sealed containers and transported in a cooler bag or box with plenty of ice bricks to keep it well chilled and fresh.

BARBECUED PRAWNS WITH LIME MAYONNAISE

picture page 61

serves: 6   prep: 30 mins   cooking: 4–6 mins

24 (about 1kg) green medium king prawns
Salt & ground black pepper, to taste
Olive oil, for greasing

lime mayonnaise

2 egg yolks
1½ tbs fresh lime juice
¾ tsp Dijon mustard
200ml olive oil
Salt & ground black pepper, to taste

1 Peel and devein the prawns, leaving the tails intact. Soak 24 bamboo skewers in cold water (this will help prevent them burning) while making the mayonnaise.
2 To make mayonnaise, place egg yolks, lime juice and mustard in a food processor and process to combine. With motor running, gradually add the oil in a thin, steady stream until thick. Season with salt and pepper.
3 Thread prawns lengthways onto skewers. Season with salt and pepper.
4 Brush a barbecue plate with the oil and preheat on medium-high. Cook the prawns on preheated barbecue for 1–2 minutes each side or until just cooked through. Serve with the mayonnaise.

BARBECUED ROSEMARY & CHILLI LAMB CUTLETS

serves: 6   prep: 15 mins (+ 2 hours marinating time)   cooking: 8 mins

125ml (½ cup) extra virgin olive oil
105g (⅓ cup) jellied cranberry sauce
½ cup fresh rosemary leaves, finely chopped
6 garlic cloves, crushed
4 small fresh red chillies, deseeded, finely chopped
18 lamb cutlets, fat trimmed
Olive oil, for greasing
Salt & cracked black pepper, to taste
Bread, to serve

1 Combine the extra virgin olive oil, cranberry sauce, rosemary, garlic and chilli in a shallow glass or ceramic dish. Add the lamb and turn to coat. Cover with plastic wrap and place in the fridge for at least 2 hours to marinate.
2 Brush a barbecue plate with the olive oil and preheat on medium-high. Drain lamb, season with salt and pepper. Reserve the marinade.
3 Cook the lamb on preheated barbecue, basting occasionally with the reserved marinade, for 4 minutes each side for medium or until cooked to your liking. Serve with the bread.

CARROT & CABBAGE SALAD WITH
ORANGE TAHINI DRESSING

picture page 63

serves: 6 prep: 20 mins cooking: 4–5 mins

2 tbs sesame seeds

2 large carrots, peeled, coarsely grated

¼ small (about 250g) cabbage, finely shredded

50g snow pea sprouts, ends trimmed

orange tahini dressing

125ml (½ cup) olive oil

2 tbs fresh orange juice

1 tbs tahini

2 tsp caster sugar

Salt & ground black pepper, to taste

1 Place the sesame seeds in a non-stick frying pan over high heat. Cook, stirring often, for 4–5 minutes or until light golden. Remove from the heat and set aside.

2 Meanwhile, to make the dressing, place the oil, orange juice, tahini, sugar, salt and pepper in a screw-top jar. Shake well to combine.

3 Combine the toasted sesame seeds, carrots, cabbage and snow pea sprouts in a large bowl. Add the dressing and toss well to combine. Serve immediately.

EASY ORANGE CAKE

serves: 6 prep: 15 mins cooking: 1 hour

No, it isn't a mistake, the whole orange does go into this cake. It is best to use a thin-skinned navel orange that is around in winter and spring, as it has no seeds and very little bitter pith. If you want to take the cake on a picnic, it is easiest to pierce the warm cake with a fine skewer, then pour the hot syrup over and allow to cool. This means you will get the flavour of the syrup without having to carry it separately.

Melted butter, for greasing

1 orange, quartered, cored, seeds removed

220g (1 cup) caster sugar

125g butter, melted, cooled

2 eggs, at room temperature

225g (1½ cups) self raising flour
Vanilla ice-cream or thickened cream (optional), to serve

orange syrup

250ml (1 cup) strained orange juice

170g (½ cup) orange marmalade

80g (⅓ cup) sugar

1 Preheat oven to 180°C. Brush a round 18cm cake pan with the melted butter to lightly grease. Line the base and side of the pan with non-stick baking paper.

2 Place the orange, sugar, butter and eggs in the bowl of a food processor. Process until the orange is finely chopped. Add the flour and process until just combined.

3 Spoon the cake mixture into the prepared pan and use the back of the spoon to smooth the surface. Bake for 1 hour or until a skewer inserted in the centre of the cake comes out clean. Remove from the oven and set aside for 2–3 minutes before turning onto a wire rack.

4 Meanwhile, to make the syrup, place the orange juice, marmalade and sugar in a medium saucepan. Stir over low heat until the sugar dissolves. Increase heat to high and bring to the boil. Reduce heat to medium and boil gently, uncovered, without stirring, for 5 minutes or until the syrup reduces slightly.

5 Serve warm or at room temperature, cut into wedges and drizzled with the warm syrup. Serve with ice-cream or cream, if desired.

WATERCRESS SOUP WITH CROUTONS

PEPPERED STEAK WITH MUSHROOM SAUCE

CREAMY MASH

CELERIAC, RED CABBAGE & CELERY SALAD

SPICED CARAMELISED ORANGES
WITH MASCARPONE CREAM

A spicy shiraz from Coonawarra in South Australia would be perfect. Wynns Coonawarra and Riddoch are both always beautifully made and great value

SUMPTUOUS & SIMPLE

Unassuming but impressive, this memorable menu is a mix of interesting and familiar flavours, brought together with minimal fuss. The caramelised oranges that complete this meal are something I've been cooking for years. Versatile and easy, I know you'll love them too.

WATERCRESS SOUP WITH CROUTONS

serves: 6   prep: 20–25 mins   cooking: 25 mins

You can make this soup to the end of step 4 up to 2 days before serving. Reheat in a saucepan over medium heat until simmering and then continue from step 5 of the recipe. You can make the croutons up to 1 week ahead—keep them in an airtight container.

2   bunches (about 350g) watercress, washed, dried
20g   (1 tbs) butter
1   brown onion, diced
2   garlic cloves, crushed
2   (about 440g) pontiac potatoes, peeled, diced
1L   (4 cups) chicken or vegetable stock
    Salt & ground black pepper, to taste

croutons

4   thick slices white bread, crusts removed
40g   (2 tbs) unsalted butter, melted

1   To make the croutons, preheat oven to 180°C. Cut the bread into 1.5cm cubes and toss with the melted butter. Spread over a baking tray and cook in preheated oven, shaking the tray halfway through cooking, for 20 minutes, until golden and crisp. Set aside.

2   Reserve 12 small watercress sprigs for garnishing. Remove the leaves from the remaining stems. Discard stems and set the leaves aside.

3   Melt the butter in a medium saucepan over medium heat. Add the onion and cook, stirring often, for 5 minutes or until it softens slightly. Add garlic and cook, stirring, for 1 minute or until aromatic.

4   Stir in the potatoes and stock, cover and bring to the boil over high heat. Reduce heat to medium-low and simmer, covered, for 10 minutes or until the potatoes are very tender. Remove from the heat. (See microwave tip.)

5   Add the watercress leaves to the soup, cover and set aside for 2 minutes or until they wilt.

6   Place half the soup in the bowl of a food processor or blender and process until smooth. Transfer to a warmed serving dish. Season with salt and pepper. Repeat with the remaining soup.

7   Ladle the soup into serving bowls. Serve sprinkled with croutons and garnished with the reserved watercress sprigs.

microwave tip: place the butter, onion and garlic in a large, heatproof microwave-safe bowl. Cook, uncovered, on High/800watts/100% for 2–3 minutes or until the onion softens slightly. Add the potatoes and stock, cover with a lid or plastic wrap and cook on High/800watts/100% for 10–15 minutes or until the potatoes are very tender.

PEPPERED STEAK WITH MUSHROOM SAUCE

serves: 6   prep: 10 mins   cooking: 35 mins

50g (¼ cup) green peppercorns in brine, drained
3 tsp black peppercorns
¼ tsp salt
6 (about 2.5cm thick and 180g each) beef fillet steaks
1 tbs olive oil
50g (2½ tbs) butter
400g mushroom caps, sliced
125ml (½ cup) brandy
250ml (1 cup) beef stock
160ml (⅔ cup) thickened cream

1 Use a mortar and pestle or the flat side of a knife to coarsely crush the green peppercorns. Place in a small bowl. Crush the black peppercorns the same way, then place in a sieve and shake to remove any powdered pepper. Add to the green peppercorns with the salt, and mix to combine. Press the peppercorn mixture onto both sides of the steaks to coat.

2 Heat oil and half the butter in a large non-stick frying pan over high heat. Add 3 steaks, reduce heat to medium-high and cook for 3–4 minutes each side for medium or until cooked to your liking. Transfer to a plate and cover loosely with foil. Cook the remaining steaks.

3 Add the remaining butter to the pan and heat over medium-high heat. Add the mushrooms and cook, stirring occasionally, for 4 minutes or until just tender. Stir in the brandy and bring to the boil. Boil for 2 minutes.

4 Stir in the stock and cream, and bring to a simmer. Reduce heat to medium and simmer for 10 minutes or until the sauce reduces slightly. Add the juices from the steaks and stir to combine. Serve the steaks with the sauce spooned over.

CREAMY MASH

serves: 6   prep: 10 mins   cooking: 20 mins

1kg sebago (brushed) potatoes, peeled
2 garlic cloves, peeled
125ml (½ cup) milk
80g butter, cubed
Salt & ground black pepper, to taste

1 Cut the potatoes into 3cm chunks. Place in a large saucepan and cover with cold water. Bring to the boil over high heat. Reduce heat to medium-high and boil gently, partially covered, for 10 minutes or until soft. (Test by piercing the potatoes with a skewer.) Drain in a colander and set aside for 5 minutes to cool slightly and dry.

2 Meanwhile, bruise the garlic cloves by pressing down on them with the flat side of a knife. Place in a small saucepan with the milk and bring just to a simmer over low heat. Remove from the heat and set aside.

3 Return the potatoes to the dry saucepan and place over medium-low heat. Use a potato masher to partially mash the potatoes. Add the butter and mash until smooth.

4 Remove the garlic from the milk and discard. Add half the milk to the potatoes and use a wooden spoon to beat vigorously until smooth. Add the remaining milk and beat until light and fluffy. Season well with salt and pepper, and serve immediately.

CELERIAC, RED CABBAGE & CELERY SALAD

serves: 6   prep: 10 mins

Celeriac is one of those vegetables that discolour once the flesh is exposed to the air. The best way to prevent this, if you wish to peel it some time before grating and serving, is to put it in a bowl of water with a little lemon juice.

1 small (about 400g) celeriac, trimmed
4 celery sticks, thinly diagonally sliced
⅛ small (about 150g) red cabbage, finely shredded
Salt & ground black pepper, to taste

parsley & caper dressing
80ml (⅓ cup) canola oil
1 tbs fresh lemon juice
1 tbs capers, drained
¼ cup firmly packed fresh continental parsley leaves

1 To make the dressing, place the oil, lemon juice, capers and parsley in the bowl of a food processor. Process until well combined and the capers and parsley are finely chopped.

2 Peel and coarsely grate the celeriac. Combine the celeriac, celery and cabbage in a large bowl. Add the dressing and gently toss the vegetables to coat. Taste and season with salt and pepper, if necessary. Serve immediately.

SPICED CARAMELISED ORANGES WITH MASCARPONE CREAM

serves: 6   prep: 10 mins (+ 1–2 hours standing time)   cooking: 15–20 mins

335g   (1½ cups) sugar

125ml   (½ cup) water

3   star anise

1   large cinnamon stick, broken in half

6   oranges

mascarpone cream

1   egg white, at room temperature

1   250g container mascarpone

2 tsp   brown sugar

1   Combine the sugar and water in a medium saucepan and stir over low heat until the sugar dissolves. Add the star anise and cinnamon, and bring to the boil over high heat.

2   Reduce heat to medium and boil, uncovered, without stirring, for 10–15 minutes or until golden. Brush down the side of the pan occasionally with a wet pastry brush to remove any sugar crystals.

3   Meanwhile, peel oranges and remove any pith. Cut into 1cm-thick rounds and arrange, slightly overlapping, in a shallow heatproof dish.

4   When toffee is ready, remove from heat and set aside for 1–2 minutes or until bubbles subside. Pour evenly over oranges, cover with a tea towel and set aside for 1–2 hours or until toffee partially dissolves.

5   To make the mascarpone cream, use a balloon whisk to whisk the egg white in a clean, dry medium bowl until soft peaks form. Use a metal spoon to soften the mascarpone if necessary, then add to the egg white with the sugar and fold in until just combined. Cover and place in the fridge until required.

6   Serve the oranges with their toffee and syrup, and mascarpone cream.

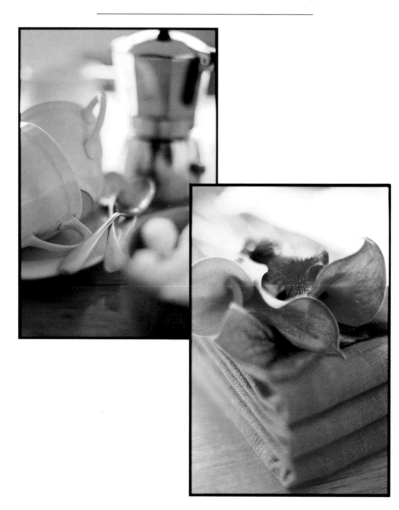

FIGS WRAPPED IN PROSCIUTTO

LEMON & TUNA SPAGHETTI WITH ANCHOVY BREADCRUMBS

ROCKET & PARMESAN SALAD

PANNA COTTA WITH COFFEE SYRUP & GRILLED PEACHES

*Try an Aussie-made, Italian-style
wine like the Montrose Sangiovese
(the chianti grape) from Mudgee in New South Wales
or the same variety from Pizzini in Victoria*

AL FRESCO

Fragrant figs, salty parmesan, gutsy tuna, tart lemons, peppery rocket and pungent coffee make this menu undisputably Italian. Fresh and uncomplicated, this food is ideal for outdoor eating late into a warm afternoon.

A quick tip for making parmesan shavings is to use a vegetable peeler.

FIGS WRAPPED IN PROSCIUTTO

picture page 73

serves: 6   prep: 10 mins

24 thin prosciutto slices, excess fat removed
12 firm, ripe figs, washed, halved
1 tbs balsamic vinegar
1 tbs extra virgin olive oil
Ground black pepper, to taste

1 Wrap a slice of prosciutto around each fig half and place on a serving platter or individual plates.
2 Drizzle the figs evenly with the vinegar and oil. Sprinkle with the pepper and serve immediately.

ROCKET & PARMESAN SALAD

serves: 6   prep: 10 mins

2 small bunches (about 230g) rocket, washed, dried
100g piece parmesan, shaved
1½ tbs red wine vinegar
60ml (¼ cup) extra virgin olive oil
Salt & ground black pepper, to taste

1 Trim rocket stems. Place in a large serving bowl with the parmesan.
2 Use a fork to whisk the vinegar and oil until well combined. Season with salt and pepper. Pour over the salad and serve immediately.

LEMON & TUNA SPAGHETTI WITH ANCHOVY BREADCRUMBS

serves: 6   prep: 20 mins   cooking: 12 mins

500g dried thin spaghetti
185ml (¾ cup) extra virgin olive oil
8 drained anchovy fillets, chopped
45g (1 cup) fresh white breadcrumbs (made from Italian-style bread if possible)
600g tuna steaks (each about 2.5cm thick)
3 lemons
1 bunch green shallots, trimmed, thinly sliced
2 large garlic cloves, finely chopped
½ cup finely chopped fresh continental parsley
½ cup finely chopped fresh basil
Salt & ground black pepper, to taste

1 Cook spaghetti in a large saucepan of salted boiling water, following packet directions, until al dente. Drain, return to pan and cover.
2 Meanwhile, heat 2 tbs of the oil in a large non-stick frying pan over medium heat. Add anchovies and cook, stirring often, for 1 minute or until they break down. Add breadcrumbs and cook, stirring often, for 3 minutes or until golden and crisp. Transfer to a plate and set aside.
3 Wipe the pan with paper towel, then add 1 tbs of the remaining oil and heat over medium-high heat. Add tuna and cook for 2–3 minutes each side or until almost cooked through. Transfer to a plate and cover loosely with foil. (The tuna will continue to cook on standing.)
4 Use a zester to remove the rind from 2 of the lemons. (Alternatively, use a vegetable peeler to peel the rind. Use a small, sharp knife to remove the white pith, then cut the rind into very thin strips.) Juice all the lemons.
5 Combine the remaining 125ml (½ cup) oil with the lemon rind, lemon juice, green shallots, garlic, parsley, basil and 1 tsp salt in a large bowl. Season with pepper, to taste. Add the drained spaghetti and toss well to combine.
6 Break the tuna into bite-sized chunks, add to the pasta and toss gently to distribute evenly. Serve warm or at room temperature, sprinkled with the anchovy breadcrumbs.

PANNA COTTA WITH COFFEE SYRUP & GRILLED PEACHES

serves: 6   prep: 20 mins (+ 6 hours setting time)   cooking: 50 mins

If I had to choose a 'Last Supper', this dessert would be the finale. I adore panna cotta
but this recipe is extra special. Silky smooth with a hint of coffee, it makes the perfect partner for a sweet
summer peach. Harmonious and heavenly!

Vegetable oil, for greasing
600ml thickened cream
125ml (½ cup) milk
115g (½ cup) caster sugar
2 tsp espresso coffee beans
1 tsp vanilla essence
1 tbs boiling water
2½ tsp powdered gelatine
6 just-ripe, small freestone peaches
1 tbs icing sugar, sifted

coffee syrup
500ml (2 cups) water
115g (½ cup) caster sugar
25g (½ cup) espresso coffee beans

1 Brush six 125ml (½-cup) metal or plastic dariole moulds with the oil to lightly grease. Place the cream, milk, sugar, coffee beans and vanilla essence in a medium heavy-based saucepan. Cook over low heat, stirring often, for 20 minutes (don't let it boil). Remove from the heat and strain through a fine sieve into a medium bowl.

2 Place the boiling water in a small heatproof bowl. Sprinkle with the gelatine and whisk well with a fork to remove any lumps.

Set aside for 3 minutes or until the gelatine dissolves and the mixture is clear.

3 Fill a large bowl with ice cubes. Gradually whisk the gelatine mixture into the cream mixture. Place the bowl on the ice, whisking occasionally, for about 10 minutes or until the mixture thickens and coats the back of a wooden spoon.

4 Spoon the mixture evenly into the greased moulds and place on a tray. Cover the tray with plastic wrap and place in the fridge for at least 6 hours to set.

5 Meanwhile, to make the syrup, place the water, sugar and coffee beans in a small saucepan. Stir over low heat until the sugar dissolves. Increase heat to medium-high and bring to the boil, stirring occasionally. Reduce heat to medium and simmer, uncovered, for 20 minutes or until thickened slightly. Remove from the heat and strain into a heatproof jug. Set aside for 30 minutes or until the syrup has cooled to room temperature.

6 Preheat grill on high. Halve the peaches and remove the stones. Place the peach halves, cut-side up, on a baking tray lined with foil. Dust with the icing sugar and cook under preheated grill for 2–3 minutes or until golden. Cut into quarters and peel away the skin.

7 To serve, remove panna cotta from the moulds by dipping 1 mould at a time in hot water for a few seconds, then turning onto serving plates. Spoon the coffee syrup over and serve with grilled peaches.

CHICKEN & LEEK PIES

WARM SPINACH & WALNUT SALAD

CRUSTY BREAD ROLLS

SWEET ROASTED APPLES WITH
CARDAMOM-INFUSED CUSTARD

ALMOND & ORANGE THINS

---

*Chicken and leek pie always equals chardonnay,
and a great region for this variety is Padthaway
in South Australia. Two of the best producers are
Lindemans Padthaway Vineyard
and Orlando's St Hilary*

BUDGET-FRIENDLY

These chicken and leek pies are good, really good. They hold centre stage in this 'friendly' menu—budget-friendly and host-friendly. Nobody will guess you've been watching your pennies when you bring this meal to the table. Nor will they believe how much time you can spend with your guests—all the recipes need is a few minor last-minute touches.

CHICKEN & LEEK PIES

picture page 79

serves: 8   prep: 1 hour (+ 6 hours chilling and 2 hours cooling time)   cooking: 2 hours 20 mins

You can cook the chickens for the filling up to 2 days before serving. Finish the filling up to 1 day ahead, ready for the final cooking just before serving.

2   1.5kg (size 15) chickens, rinsed, dried
2   carrots, unpeeled, chopped
1   brown onion, unpeeled, quartered
6   celery sticks, thinly sliced
2   bay leaves
2L   (8 cups) water, approximately
720g   (about 4) desiree potatoes, peeled, cut into 2cm pieces
150g   butter
3   large leeks, trimmed, halved lengthways, washed, thinly sliced
115g   (¾ cup) plain flour
250ml   (1 cup) milk
    Salt & ground black pepper, to taste
8   sheets (25 x 25cm) ready-rolled frozen puff pastry, partially thawed
24   fresh thyme sprigs (about ½ bunch)
1   egg, lightly whisked
8   crusty bread rolls, to serve

1   Use kitchen scissors or poultry shears to cut the chickens in half lengthways. Place the chickens, carrots, onion, ½ cup of the sliced celery and the bay leaves in a large stockpot. Add the water, making sure the chicken is completely covered (add a little more water if necessary). Cover and bring to the boil over high heat. Reduce heat to medium-low and cook, covered, for 1 hour.

2   Transfer chickens to a large plate. Set aside for 20 minutes or until cool enough to handle. Use your hands to remove the meat, discard the skin and bones. Roughly chop the meat and place in an airtight container in the fridge until required.

3   Strain the stock and return to the stockpot. Bring to the boil over high heat. Boil, uncovered, for 25 minutes or until stock reduces to about 750ml (3 cups). Set aside until cooled completely, then transfer to an airtight container. Place in the fridge for at least 6 hours.

4   Use a slotted spoon to remove any fat from the surface of the stock. Bring a medium saucepan of water to the boil over high heat. Add the potatoes and cook for 10 minutes or until just tender. Drain well.

5   Meanwhile, melt 30g (1½ tbs) of the butter in a large saucepan over medium-high heat. Add the remaining celery and the leeks, and cook, stirring often, for 4–5 minutes or until they are just soft. Use a slotted spoon to transfer to a bowl.

6   Melt the remaining 120g butter in the pan over medium-high heat until foaming. Add the flour and use a wooden spoon to stir well. Combine 750ml (3 cups) of stock and the milk in a large jug. Remove pan from heat and gradually stir in stock mixture until smooth. Return to medium-high heat, stirring constantly, for 10–12 minutes or until sauce thickens and comes to the boil. Taste and season with salt and pepper. Remove from heat and stir in the potatoes, celery and leeks, and chicken. Place in the fridge for 1 hour or until chilled.

7   Preheat oven to 220°C. You will need eight 500ml (2-cup) heatproof dishes or bowls, about 12.5cm in diameter (top measurement). Place pastry on a clean surface. Using the top of a dish as a guide, cut a disc about 2cm larger than the dish (all the way round) from each sheet. Spoon the chicken mixture evenly into the dishes and press 3 thyme sprigs into each. Lightly brush rims of the dishes with water. Top each with a pastry disc and press pastry against rim of the dish to seal. Cut a cross in the top of each and brush lightly with whisked egg.

8   Place the pies on 2 baking trays and bake in preheated oven for 20–25 minutes or until heated through and the pastry is puffed and golden. Serve immediately with the bread rolls.

WARM SPINACH & WALNUT SALAD

serves: 8   prep: 15 mins   cooking: 5–8 mins

400g   baby spinach leaves, trimmed, washed, dried
    Salt & ground black pepper, to taste

    warm walnut dressing
125ml   (½ cup) olive oil
200g   walnut pieces, roughly chopped
2 tbs   fresh lemon juice

1   Place the spinach leaves in a large heatproof bowl.

2   To make the dressing, heat the oil in a medium frying pan over medium-high heat. Add the walnuts and cook, tossing often, for 4–5 minutes or until lightly toasted. Remove from the heat and stir in the lemon juice.

3   Pour the dressing over the spinach. Season with salt and plenty of ground black pepper, and toss gently to combine. Serve immediately.

SWEET ROASTED APPLES WITH CARDAMOM-INFUSED CUSTARD

serves: 8   prep: 30 mins   cooking: 40–50 mins

80g (½ cup) pure icing sugar
½ tsp ground cinnamon
8 (about 200g each) apples (like golden delicious)

cardamom-infused custard
300ml thin cream
250ml (1 cup) milk
3 tsp cardamom seeds
6 egg yolks
60g (¼ cup) caster sugar
1 tsp cornflour

1 To make the custard, heat the cream, milk and cardamom seeds in a medium heavy-based saucepan over low heat, stirring occasionally, for 30 minutes or until the mixture just reaches boiling point. Strain through a fine sieve into a heatproof jug. Discard cardamom seeds.

2 Meanwhile, place an oven rack in the centre of the oven and another rack in the position above. Preheat oven to 220°C. Line 2 shallow baking trays with non-stick baking paper.

3 Combine the icing sugar and cinnamon. Working quickly (so the apples don't discolour), use an apple corer to core the apples and then cut each apple into 5 thick rings. Place the apple rings in a single layer on the lined trays.

4 Sift half the icing sugar mixture over the apple rings, then turn the rings and sift the remaining mixture over the top. Use a pastry brush to brush the apple rings with any icing sugar mixture remaining on the baking paper.

5 Bake in preheated oven, swapping trays halfway through cooking, for 35–40 minutes or until tender and just golden around the edges.

6 Meanwhile, to finish the custard, use electric beaters to whisk the egg yolks, sugar and cornflour in a large bowl until light and foaming.

7 Return to a clean saucepan and use a wooden spoon to stir over medium-low heat for 15–18 minutes or until the custard thickens and coats the back of the spoon. Strain through a fine sieve into a heatproof jug.

8 Remove the apples from the oven and turn on the trays to coat in the liquid. Serve immediately with the custard.

ALMOND & ORANGE THINS

makes: about 45   prep: 30 mins (+ 2 hours cooling time)
cooking: 1¼ hours

Melted butter, for greasing
3 egg whites, at room temperature
115g (½ cup) caster sugar
100g almond kernels
1 tbs finely grated orange rind
115g (¾ cup) plain flour

1 Preheat oven to 180°C. Brush a 9 x 22cm bar pan with the butter to grease. Line with non-stick baking paper, letting it overhang the sides.

2 Use electric beaters to whisk the egg whites in a clean, dry large bowl until soft peaks form. Add the sugar 1 tbs at a time, whisking well after each addition until the sugar dissolves.

3 Use a large metal spoon to fold in the almonds and orange rind. Sift the flour over the egg white mixture and fold in until combined.

4 Spoon into prepared pan and smooth surface. Bake in preheated oven for 40–45 minutes or until firm and cooked through. Remove from pan, discard paper and place on a wire rack for 1½ hours to cool.

5 Preheat oven to 140°C. Use a serrated knife to cut the loaf into 5mm-thick slices. Place the slices in a single layer on 2 baking trays. Bake in preheated oven, swapping the trays halfway through cooking, for 30 minutes or until dry and crisp. Allow to cool on the trays.

WEEKEND DINNERS

With the pace slowing a little on the weekends, it is often when we are most at ease to invite friends and family for a home-cooked meal.

Choose a theme and create a mood to complement your food—Thai, Sicilian or Indian. Dress your outdoor table with fresh colours and enjoy a twilight dinner on a balmy summer's night. Or gather inside, warm and cosy, on giant cushions for comfort. The menus that follow are filled with fabulous ideas for simple and successful weekend dinners.

STEAMED WATER CHESTNUT,
SPINACH & MUSHROOM DUMPLINGS

FRAGRANT ROAST CHICKEN
WITH CORIANDER POTATOES

SESAME BEANS

BROWN-SUGARED PINEAPPLE

---

*Food with a twist, so why not choose a wine to
match—St Huberts Roussanne is one of a kind,
a white that will further excite your tastebuds.
Otherwise, a classic aged riesling like Leo Buring's
Leonay would be delicious*

SUNDAY NIGHT ROAST (WITH A TWIST)

*When I was growing up, roast chicken was
always the 'special occasion' meal. This menu
gives this familiar favourite a fresh make-over,
with coriander, lemon grass, kaffir lime leaves
and snake beans adding a clever Asian twist.
Try serving the meal with green tea and
finishing with fortune cookies.*

STEAMED WATER CHESTNUT, SPINACH & MUSHROOM DUMPLINGS

picture page 89

serves: 4   prep: 20 mins   cooking: 10 mins

1 tbs   peanut oil
2   garlic cloves, crushed
5cm   piece fresh ginger, peeled, grated
4   medium shiitake mushrooms, finely chopped
8   drained canned water chestnuts, finely chopped
8   medium English spinach leaves, roughly chopped
2 tsp   chopped fresh coriander leaves
12   flour wonton wrappers
Soy sauce, for dipping

1   Line the base of a 25cm bamboo steamer with non-stick baking paper. Heat the oil in a medium frying pan over medium heat. Add the garlic, ginger and mushrooms, and stir over medium heat for 1–2 minutes or until the mushrooms are tender.

2   Remove pan from heat. Add the water chestnuts, spinach and coriander, and stir until the spinach wilts.

3   Place a wonton wrapper on a work surface and spoon about 1½ tsp of the mushroom mixture into the centre. Use your finger to wet the edges of the wrapper with a little water. Bring the edges together and press firmly together to enclose the filling and form a pouch. Repeat with the remaining wrappers and filling.

4   Bring 5cm of water to the boil in a wok. Reduce heat to medium. Place the wontons in the lined steamer and cover with a tight-fitting lid (place a clean tea towel over the steamer before covering with the lid if it is a little loose). Place the steamer in the wok, making sure it doesn't touch the water. Steam for 4–5 minutes or until the wonton wrappers are tender and the filling is heated through. Serve with the soy sauce, for dipping.

FRAGRANT ROAST CHICKEN WITH CORIANDER POTATOES

serves: 4   prep: 20 mins   cooking: 1 hour

1   1.8kg (size 18) chicken
1   lemon grass stem, pale section only, finely chopped
3   garlic cloves, finely chopped
4   kaffir lime leaves, centre vein removed, finely shredded
60ml   (¼ cup) peanut oil
Salt & ground black pepper, to taste
12   (about 500g) chat (small coliban) potatoes
2 tbs   chopped fresh coriander

1   Preheat oven to 220°C. Line the base of a large roasting pan with non-stick baking paper.

2   Briefly rinse the chicken cavity with cold running water. Pat the chicken dry with paper towel (both inside and out).

3   Combine the lemon grass, garlic, lime leaves and 1 tbs of the oil in a small bowl. Season with salt and pepper. Use your fingers to loosen the skin from the flesh of the chicken on the breast and legs (take care not to break the skin), then spread the lemon grass mixture evenly over the flesh of the chicken.

4   Place 1 tbs of remaining oil in a small bowl and season with salt and pepper. Rub seasoned oil into chicken's skin. Place remaining 1 tbs oil in a large bowl and add potatoes. Season with salt and toss to coat.

5   Place the chicken in the lined pan and arrange the potatoes around it. Roast in preheated oven for 1 hour or until the chicken is just cooked through and the juices run clear when pierced with a skewer in the thickest part of the breast.

6   Remove the potatoes from the pan and place in a large bowl with the coriander. Toss to combine. Place the chicken and potatoes on a platter and serve immediately.

SESAME BEANS

serves: 4   prep: 5 mins   cooking: 5 mins

Regular green beans will work equally well in this recipe. Use them instead of the snake beans and simply trim the tops before cooking.

2 tsp   peanut oil
2   garlic cloves, crushed
1   bunch (about 300g) snake beans, ends trimmed, cut into 10cm lengths
1 tsp   sesame oil

1   Heat the peanut oil in a large frying pan or wok over medium heat. Add the garlic and snake beans. Cook, tossing often, for 3–4 minutes or until the beans are tender and bright green.

2   Remove from the heat, add the sesame oil and toss to coat. Serve immediately.

BROWN-SUGARED PINEAPPLE

serves: 4   prep: 5 mins   cooking: 12–17 mins

The aroma of a pineapple is the best indicator of its quality and ripeness.
A good one will have a pleasant, sweet fragrance. Remember, pineapples don't continue to ripen
once picked, but do deteriorate, so eat them as soon as possible. You can serve this dessert with
frozen vanilla yoghurt instead of the ice-cream.

40g (2 tbs) butter

1 small pineapple, peeled, cut into
1cm-thick slices, halved

45g (¼ cup, lightly packed) brown sugar

Vanilla ice-cream, to serve

1 Melt the butter in a large frying pan over medium heat. Add the pineapple and brown sugar, and toss well.

2 Cook, turning occasionally, for 10-15 minutes or until the liquid reduces to a sauce consistency and the pineapple is golden.

3 Serve immediately with scoops of ice-cream.

variation: GLAZED APPLES WITH PECAN NUTS

Place 45g (⅓ cup) pecan nuts in a frying pan over medium heat. Cook, stirring, for 2–3 minutes or until lightly toasted. Transfer to a chopping board and roughly chop. Set aside. Replace the pineapple with 3 large pink lady or golden delicious apples. Peel, core and halve the apples, then cut into 2cm-thick slices. Cook for 12 minutes, then serve sprinkled with the pecan nuts.

OLIVE, ARTICHOKE & SPINACH PIZZA

ICE-CREAM WITH ESPRESSO & FRANGELICO

For an impromptu dinner, you want a cheap and cheery bottle of red—they come no better than the classic Jacob's Creek Shiraz Cabernet or Rosemount's New Australian Red

AT THE LAST MINUTE

This menu is ideal for last-minute get-togethers. The clever 'throw-together' recipes use stand-by ingredients to their best advantage. Once served and enjoyed, it's hard to believe just how easy they are to prepare.

OLIVE, ARTICHOKE & SPINACH PIZZA

serves: 4   prep: 10 mins   cooking: 20 mins

2   (30cm-diameter) bought pizza bases
70g   (¼ cup) bought olive tapenade
8   (about 450g) artichoke hearts in oil, drained, quartered
8   thin slices (about 150g) prosciutto, quartered
100g   (1 cup) coarsely grated mozzarella
60g   baby spinach leaves
Ground black pepper, to taste

1   Preheat oven to 220°C.
2   Place the pizza bases on 2 oven or pizza trays and spread the tapenade evenly over each. Arrange the artichokes and prosciutto on top and sprinkle evenly with the mozzarella.
3   Bake in preheated oven, swapping trays halfway through cooking, for 20 minutes or until the bases are crisp and cheese begins to brown. Transfer to a chopping board. Cut each pizza into 6 wedges and top with the spinach leaves. Sprinkle with pepper and serve immediately.

variation: ITALIAN SAUSAGE, RICOTTA & OLIVE PIZZA

Replace the tapenade with bought sun-dried tomato paste. Omit the artichoke hearts and prosciutto. Heat 1 tbs olive oil in a non-stick frying pan over medium heat and cook 3 (about 260g) thin, Italian-style sausages for 10 minutes or until cooked through. Cut into 1cm-thick slices. Sprinkle the mozzarella over the sun-dried tomato paste, then top with the sausages; 145g (¾ cup) kalamata olives, halved and pitted; and 160g fresh ricotta, broken into bite-sized pieces. Cook as above and top with the spinach leaves before serving.

ICE-CREAM WITH ESPRESSO & FRANGELICO

serves: 4   prep: 5 mins (+ 3–5 mins standing time)

I always serve this dessert when I don't have time to cook. There are no secrets to this one—
just good-quality ice-cream and strong coffee with a generous splash of Frangelico.

25g (¼ cup) ground espresso coffee

375ml (1½ cups) boiling water

8 scoops vanilla ice-cream

60ml (¼ cup) Frangelico

1 Place the coffee in a plunger and add the boiling water. Set aside for 3–5 minutes to brew. Plunge.

2 Place ice-cream in 4 heatproof serving glasses, cups or bowls, and pour Frangelico over each. Pass coffee around to pour over the top.

variation: ICE-CREAM WITH COFFEE & CHOCOLATE
Sprinkle the ice-cream with 45g (⅓ cup) coarsely grated, good-quality
dark chocolate before pouring the Frangelico and coffee over.

SPICED PRAWNS WITH CURRY LEAVES

COCONUT CHICKEN CURRY

VEGETABLES IN SPICED YOGHURT

STEAMED BASMATI RICE

PAPPADUMS

RICE & CARDAMOM DESSERT

*Why not try a fresh, slightly sweet style of white,
like the classic Wyndham Estate TR2 Select White or
Brown Brothers Spätlese Lexia*

INDIAN FEAST

*At the heart of Indian cuisine are wonderful
spice combinations. This menu has been
inspired by the exotic food of southern India
which is full of earthy tones and spicy
characters, with a tropical twist. The layered
flavours and aromatic qualities of these dishes
will give you a true taste of India.*

SPICED PRAWNS WITH CURRY LEAVES

serves: 8   prep: 20–25 mins (+ 1–6 hours marinating time)   cooking: 15–18 mins

*You can marinate the prawns and cook the mustard-seed mixture up to 6 hours before serving. Keep in separate airtight containers in the fridge.
Cook the prawns just before serving. Curry leaves are available from some supermarkets, greengrocers and Asian food stores*

40 (about 1.7kg) green medium prawns,
 peeled with tails left intact, deveined

2 tbs vegetable oil

1 tsp brown mustard seeds

4 green shallots, pale section only, shredded

15 fresh curry leaves (optional)

marinade

2 tbs fresh lime juice

1 tbs vegetable oil

1 tsp chilli powder

1 tsp ground coriander

1 tsp ground turmeric

6 green shallots, trimmed, finely chopped

1 tsp finely grated fresh ginger

2 garlic cloves, crushed
 Salt & ground black pepper, to taste

1 To make the marinade, combine the lime juice, oil, chilli powder, coriander, turmeric, green shallots, ginger, garlic, salt and pepper in a large glass or ceramic bowl and mix well. Add the prawns and stir well to coat in the marinade. Cover and place in the fridge for at least 1 hour (or up to 6 hours) for the flavours to develop.

2 Heat 1 tbs of the oil in a large frying pan or wok over medium heat. Add the mustard seeds and cook, stirring, for 30 seconds or until they begin to pop. Add the green shallots and curry leaves, and cook, stirring, for 2 minutes or until the green shallots begin to brown. Transfer to a bowl and set aside.

3 Heat the remaining 1 tbs of oil in the pan or wok over medium-high heat. Add a third of the prawns and cook, tossing often, for 3–4 minutes or until they curl, change colour and are just cooked through. Transfer to a plate and set aside. Repeat with the remaining prawns in 2 more batches.

4 Return prawns to pan with mustard-seed mixture. Toss over medium heat for 1 minute or until just heated through. Serve immediately.

PAPPADUMS

You will need 2–3 pappadums per person for this menu. One of the easiest ways to cook them is in the microwave oven. To do this, place 4 pappadums at a time on a heatproof, microwave-safe rack or plate lined with non-stick baking paper. Cook, uncovered, on High/800watts/100% for 1–2 minutes or until they expand and crumple. Repeat with remaining pappadums.

COCONUT CHICKEN CURRY

serves: 8   prep: 20 mins   cooking: 35–40 mins

60ml (¼ cup) vegetable oil

2 tsp brown mustard seeds

1 brown onion, cut into thin wedges

2 garlic cloves, thinly sliced

2cm piece fresh ginger, peeled, cut into thin strips

15 fresh curry leaves (optional)

3 tsp ground coriander

1 tsp ground turmeric

½ tsp chilli powder

Salt & ground black pepper, to taste

8 (about 800g) chicken thigh fillets, trimmed, halved

1 400ml can coconut milk

2 tsp white vinegar

1 small fresh red chilli, halved, deseeded, thinly sliced

2 limes, cut into wedges, to serve

1 Heat 2 tbs of the oil in a large saucepan over medium heat. Add the mustard seeds and cook, stirring, for 30 seconds or until they begin to pop. Add the onion, reduce heat to low and cook, stirring occasionally, for 8 minutes or until it is soft.

2 Stir in the garlic, ginger, curry leaves, coriander, turmeric, chilli powder, salt and pepper, and cook, stirring, for 1 minute or until aromatic. Transfer the mixture to a bowl and set aside.

3 Heat the remaining 1 tbs of oil in the saucepan over medium-high heat. Add half the chicken thighs and cook, tossing occasionally, for 5 minutes or until sealed. Transfer to a plate and repeat with the remaining chicken thighs.

4 Return the onion mixture and chicken to the pan over medium-high heat. Add the coconut milk, vinegar and fresh chilli. Bring to the boil, then reduce heat to medium-low. Simmer, covered, for 15–20 minutes or until the chicken is tender. Serve with the lime wedges.

VEGETABLES IN SPICED YOGHURT

serves: 8   prep: 15 mins   cooking: 20 mins

You can make this recipe to the end of step 3 up to 8 hours before serving. Keep the vegetables and spiced yoghurt in separate airtight containers in the fridge. Simmer the vegetables over medium heat for 1–2 minutes before continuing with step 4.

1 large desiree potato, peeled

1 large carrot, peeled

1 large zucchini

1 baby eggplant

310ml (1¼ cups) water

4 large fresh green chillies, quartered lengthways, deseeded

10 fresh curry leaves (optional)

½ tsp ground turmeric

1 brown onion, cut into thin wedges

125g green beans, topped, cut into 5cm lengths

spiced yoghurt

130g (½ cup) thick natural yoghurt

½ tsp ground coriander

½ tsp ground cumin

Salt & ground black pepper, to taste

1 Cut the potato, carrot, zucchini and eggplant into 5cm-long sticks.

2 Combine water, chillies, curry leaves and turmeric in a large saucepan and bring to the boil over medium-high heat. Stir in vegetable sticks, onion and beans. Cover, reduce heat to medium-low and simmer, stirring occasionally, for 15 minutes or until the vegetables are tender.

3 Meanwhile, to make the spiced yoghurt, combine the yoghurt, coriander and cumin in a bowl. Season well with salt and pepper.

4 Drain the vegetables, leaving about 1 tbs liquid. Add spiced yoghurt and stir gently over low heat until heated through. Serve immediately.

STEAMED BASMATI RICE

serves: 8   prep: 1 min (+ 10 mins standing time)   cooking: 20–25 mins

1.25L (5 cups) water
600g (3 cups) basmati rice

1 Bring the water to the boil in a medium heavy-based saucepan over high heat.

2 Add the rice, stir well and return to the boil. Reduce heat to very low, cover with a tight-fitting lid and cook gently for 15–20 minutes or until the water is absorbed and the rice is tender. (See microwave tip.)

3 Remove the pan from the heat and set aside, covered, for 10 minutes. Use a fork to separate the grains, and serve.

note: it is not safe to cook rice in the microwave with more than 750ml (3 cups) of liquid at a time. As a result, you will need to cook this quantity of rice in 2 batches.

microwave tip: place half each of the water and rice in a deep, 3-litre (12-cup) heatproof microwave-safe bowl or rice cooker. Cover with a lid or double layer of plastic wrap and cook on High/800watts/100% for 5 minutes, followed by Medium/500watts/50% for 9 minutes. Transfer to a large bowl, cover to keep warm and repeat with the remaining water and rice.

RICE & CARDAMOM DESSERT

serves: 8   prep: 5 mins (+ 30 mins standing time)   cooking: 30 mins

Traditionally called 'payasam', this dessert can also be based on vermicelli noodles or semolina. It can be made up to 8 hours ahead—cover and keep at room temperature. Reheat in a saucepan, covered, over low heat for 2–4 minutes or until warmed through, adding extra milk if needed.

2 tsp ghee or butter
110g (⅔ cup) unsalted raw cashew nuts
1.5L (6 cups) milk
220g (1 cup) medium-grain or arborio rice
115g (½ cup) caster sugar
1 tsp ground cardamom
65g (⅓ cup) sultanas

1 Melt the ghee or butter in a medium saucepan over medium heat. Add the cashews and cook, stirring, for 1–2 minutes or until golden. Transfer to a bowl and set aside.

2 Add the milk, rice, sugar and cardamom to the pan, stir and bring to the boil over medium-high heat. Reduce heat to low and simmer gently, uncovered, for 25 minutes or until the rice is tender and about two-thirds of the liquid is absorbed. (See microwave tip.)

3 Remove from the heat and stir in the cashews and sultanas. Set aside, covered, at room temperature for 30 minutes or until the excess liquid is absorbed. Serve lukewarm.

microwave tip: (see note above). Place half each of the milk, rice, sugar and cardamom in a deep, 2-litre (8-cup) heatproof microwave-safe bowl or rice cooker. Cover with a lid or double layer of plastic wrap and cook on High/800watts/100% for 5 minutes, followed by Medium/500watts/50% for 7 minutes or until rice is tender and about two-thirds of the liquid is absorbed. Transfer to a bowl, cover and repeat with remaining ingredients.

SOMETHING SIMPLE

I first made this fuss-free menu for friends after returning from some local markets with the best of the winter season. My bag was filled with succulent watercress, juicy ripe pears, plump ruby beetroot, aromatic fennel and tasty desiree potatoes—this is what I whipped up.

WATERCRESS, PEAR & BLUE CHEESE SALAD

serves: 6   prep: 10 mins

2   pears (like williams or packham)

1   bunch (about 310g) watercress

100g   blue cheese (like King Island
Roaring Forties), crumbled
Ground black pepper, to taste

dressing

60ml   (¼ cup) olive oil

1½ tbs   cider vinegar
Salt & ground black pepper, to taste

1   To make the dressing, place the oil, vinegar, salt and pepper in a small screw-top jar. Shake well to combine.

2   Quarter, core and slice the pears to make wedges. Place in a large bowl with the watercress. Add the dressing and toss well to combine. Divide among serving plates or bowls, then sprinkle with the blue cheese and a little pepper. Serve immediately.

LAMB WITH ROASTED VEGETABLES & BEETROOT PUREE

serves: 6   prep: 30 mins   cooking: 50–55 mins

4   large (about 1kg) desiree potatoes, unpeeled,
    halved, cut into 1cm-thick slices

2 tbs   olive oil
        Salt & ground black pepper, to taste

3   (about 300g) fennel bulbs, trimmed,
    cut lengthways into 1cm-thick slices

3   leeks, pale section only, halved crossways,
    then halved lengthways

3   (about 350g each) lamb eye of loin (backstraps)

beetroot puree

4   (about 800g) beetroot bulbs

60ml   (¼ cup) olive oil

1 tbs   fresh lemon juice

1   garlic clove

1 tsp   brown sugar
        Salt & ground black pepper, to taste

1   To make the beetroot puree, trim the leaves and root ends of the beetroot to about 3cm from the bulb. Wash the bulbs (take care not to break the skin). Place in a medium saucepan, cover with cold water and bring to the boil over high heat. Reduce heat to medium and cook, replenishing the boiling water when necessary, for 40–45 minutes or until very tender when tested with a skewer. (See microwave tip.) Drain the beetroot. Set aside to cool slightly.

2   Meanwhile, preheat oven to 220°C. Line 2 large baking trays with non-stick baking paper. Place the potatoes in a bowl, add 3 tsp of oil, season well with salt and toss to coat. Place the potatoes on a lined tray in a single layer. Place the fennel and leeks in the bowl, add 3 tsp of the remaining oil, season with salt and toss to coat. Place the fennel and leeks on the remaining lined tray. Roast the vegetables in preheated oven, swapping the trays halfway through cooking, for 30–40 minutes or until tender and golden around the edges.

3   About 15 minutes before the vegetables finish cooking, place the lamb in a bowl, add the remaining 2 tsp of oil and toss to coat. Season well with pepper. Heat a non-stick frying pan over high heat. Add the lamb, reduce heat to medium-high and cook for 4–5 minutes each side for medium or until cooked to your liking. Transfer the lamb to a plate, cover loosely with foil and set aside for 5 minutes to rest.

4   When the beetroot is cool enough to handle, put on rubber gloves and peel the skin. Cut the beetroot into quarters and place in the bowl of a food processor. Add the oil, lemon juice, garlic and sugar, and process until the mixture is smooth. Taste and season with salt and pepper. Transfer to a small bowl, cover to keep warm and set aside.

5   To serve, thickly slice the lamb. Place the roasted vegetables on serving plates, top with the lamb and serve accompanied by the warm beetroot puree.

microwave tip: place the beetroot in a single layer in a deep dish with 125ml (½ cup) water.
Cover with a tight-fitting lid or double layer of plastic wrap
and cook on High/800watts/100% for 12–15 minutes or until very tender.

CHOCOLATE SHORTBREAD

makes: 18   prep: 10 mins (+ 10 mins chilling time)   cooking: 15 mins

These biscuits will keep for up to 5 days in an airtight container.

125g   butter, at room temperature, cubed

60g   (⅓ cup) icing sugar, sifted

½ tsp   vanilla essence

150g   (1 cup) plain flour

1½ tbs   cocoa powder

Extra icing sugar, to dust

1   Preheat oven to 160°C. Line 2 baking trays with non-stick baking paper.

2   Use electric beaters to beat the butter, icing sugar and vanilla essence in a medium bowl until just combined.

3   Sift the flour and cocoa together. Add to the butter mixture and use a wooden spoon, and then your hands, to mix to a smooth dough. Wrap in plastic wrap and place in the fridge for 10 minutes to chill.

4   Roll heaped teaspoonsful of the dough into balls and place on the lined trays. Use your thumbs and 2 fingers to gently pinch the top half of each ball.

5   Bake in preheated oven, swapping the trays halfway through cooking, for 15 minutes or until cooked through. Set aside for 5 minutes before transferring to a wire rack to cool completely. Dust with icing sugar just before serving.

variation: CHOCOLATE & HAZELNUT SHORTBREAD

Spread 120g (¾ cup) hazelnuts over a baking tray and toast in an oven preheated to 180°C for 8 minutes or until aromatic. Remove from the oven and set aside to cool. Rub the hazelnuts between a clean tea towel to remove as much skin as possible. Chop and then add to the butter mixture with the flour and cocoa.

BAKED RICOTTA WITH CHUNKY OLIVE TAPENADE & CROSTINI

BUTTER BEAN & ARTICHOKE RAVIOLI WITH SUMMER HERBS

MINTED BEAN & CHERRY TOMATO SALAD

POACHED PEACHES & RASPBERRIES IN VANILLA SYRUP

Nothing would compare to trying a real Italian Chianti Classico from a famous producer like Frescobaldi or Antinori

VIVA VEGETARIAN

This elegant dinner is sure to turn a balmy summer's night into an unforgettable evening. Typical summer flavours like basil, tomatoes, peaches and raspberries shine in this host-friendly menu. All the dishes can be prepared ahead, leaving only the ravioli to be cooked and the salad dressed. So, sit back and relax.

BAKED RICOTTA WITH CHUNKY OLIVE TAPENADE & CROSTINI

serves: 6   prep: 20 mins (+ overnight firming and 30 mins cooling time)   cooking: 40 mins

baked ricotta

500g	piece fresh ricotta
2 tsp	extra virgin olive oil
	Salt & ground black pepper, to taste

chunky olive tapenade

250g	kalamata olives, pitted
1 tbs	drained capers
2	garlic cloves, finely chopped
3½ tbs	extra virgin olive oil
1½ tbs	fresh lemon juice
	Ground black pepper, to taste

crostini

1	30cm baguette (French stick), cut into 5mm-thick slices
	Olive oil, for brushing

1 To make the baked ricotta, line a tray with 4 layers of paper towel. Carefully place the ricotta on the lined tray and cover with 4 more layers of paper towel. Place in the fridge overnight to firm.

2 Meanwhile, to make the tapenade, place the olives, capers, garlic, oil and lemon juice in the bowl of a food processor. Process until combined and the olives are coarsely chopped. Season with pepper. Transfer to a serving bowl, cover with plastic wrap and place in the fridge until required.

3 To make the crostini, preheat oven to 200°C and line 2 baking trays with non-stick baking paper. Brush both sides of the baguette slices lightly with oil. Place on the lined trays and bake in preheated oven for 10 minutes or until light golden and crisp. Remove from the oven and allow to cool on the trays. Transfer to an airtight container until required.

4 Increase oven temperature to 220°C. Line a baking tray with non-stick baking paper. Remove all the paper towel and carefully transfer the ricotta in 1 piece to the lined tray. Drizzle with the oil and sprinkle with salt and pepper. Bake in preheated oven for 30 minutes or until firm and light golden. Remove from the oven and set aside on the tray for 30 minutes or until cooled to room temperature. Cover and place in the fridge until required.

5 Serve the ricotta at room temperature. Cut into serving portions and place on individual plates with tapenade and crostini. (Alternatively, serve the ricotta, tapenade and crostini together on a large platter.)

BUTTER BEAN & ARTICHOKE RAVIOLI WITH SUMMER HERBS

serves: 6   prep: 35 mins   cooking: 20 mins

butter bean & artichoke ravioli

1½ tbs	extra virgin olive oil
2	garlic cloves, finely chopped
1½	300g cans butter beans, rinsed, drained
2	(about 105g) marinated artichoke hearts, finely chopped
3	green shallots, trimmed, thinly sliced
2 tsp	fresh lemon juice
	Salt & ground black pepper
600g	(12) fresh lasagne sheets
1	egg, lightly whisked

summer herb sauce

125g	butter, cubed
¼ cup	finely chopped fresh continental parsley leaves
2 tbs	finely chopped fresh basil leaves
2 tbs	finely snipped fresh chives
1½ tbs	fresh lemon juice
	Salt & ground black pepper, to taste

1 To make the ravioli, place oil and garlic in a small saucepan and stir over medium heat for 1 minute or until aromatic. Remove from heat, then place in a food processor with the butter beans and process, scraping side of bowl when necessary, until coarsely pureed. Transfer to a bowl and stir in the artichokes, green shallots, lemon juice, salt and pepper.

2 Place lasagne sheets on a work surface and cover with a damp tea towel. Use a round 7.5cm cutter to cut 6 discs from each sheet. Cover with the damp tea towel once cut.

3 Brush 2 pasta discs lightly with whisked egg. Place a small spoonful of filling in the centre of one disc, then place the other disc on top and press the edges to seal and enclose the filling. Place on a tray dusted with flour and repeat with the remaining pasta discs, egg and filling. Cover with plastic wrap and place in the fridge until required.

4 To make sauce, heat the butter in a small saucepan over medium heat for 1–2 minutes or until it is just brown. Remove from the heat, stir in the herbs, lemon juice, salt and pepper, and cover to keep warm.

5 To cook ravioli, add a pinch of salt and a third of the ravioli to a large saucepan of boiling water. Stir gently, cover and return to boil. Uncover and boil for 5 minutes or until al dente. Transfer to a bowl and cover loosely with foil. Repeat with remaining ravioli. Serve with sauce.

MINTED BEAN & CHERRY TOMATO SALAD

serves: 6   prep: 10 mins   cooking: 5 mins

600g	green beans, topped
250g	(1 punnet) cherry tomatoes
2 tbs	sunflower seed kernels
1 tbs	sesame seeds

dressing

60ml	(¼ cup) olive oil
1½ tbs	fresh lemon juice
¼ cup	chopped fresh mint leaves
1	garlic clove, crushed
	Salt & ground black pepper, to taste

1 Bring a large saucepan of water to the boil over high heat. Add the beans, return to the boil and cook for 1–2 minutes or until bright green and tender crisp. Drain and refresh in iced water.

2 Drain the beans well and place in a large bowl. Add the tomatoes, sunflower seed kernels and sesame seeds, and toss to combine.

3 To make the dressing, place the oil, lemon juice, mint, garlic, salt and pepper in a small screw-top jar. Shake well to combine.

4 To serve, pour the dressing over the salad and toss gently to combine.

POACHED PEACHES & RASPBERRIES IN VANILLA SYRUP

serves: 6   prep: 10 mins (+ 20 mins cooling time)   cooking: 20 mins

Firm, ripe peaches are best for this recipe—they will hold their shape when poached and are easy to peel.
Unripe peaches are best kept at room temperature out of direct sunlight. The stem end will become a rich yellow when ripe.
Once ripe, keep them in an unsealed plastic bag in the fridge for up to 3 days.

6 medium (about 600g) firm, ripe peaches
1L (4 cups) water
335g (1½ cups) sugar
1 vanilla bean, split lengthways
1 cinnamon stick
150g (1 punnet) raspberries
Vanilla ice-cream or thickened
cream (optional), to serve

1 Use a small sharp knife to cut a shallow cross in the top or base of each peach.

2 Combine the water, sugar, vanilla bean and cinnamon stick in a saucepan large enough to hold the peaches in a single layer. Use a wooden spoon to stir over medium heat until the sugar dissolves.

3 Bring the syrup to the boil over high heat. Reduce heat to medium-low and add the peaches. Simmer gently, turning the peaches occasionally, for 5 minutes or until the skin begins to peel away and the peaches are just tender when tested with a skewer. Use a slotted spoon to transfer the peaches to a plate.

4 Increase heat to high and boil the syrup for 10 minutes or until it reduces by about half.

5 Meanwhile, peel the peaches and discard the skin. Place the peaches in a heatproof serving dish.

6 Pour the hot syrup over the peaches with the vanilla bean and cinnamon stick. Set aside for 20 minutes to cool slightly. Add the raspberries and serve warm or allow to cool to room temperature. Serve with ice-cream or cream, if desired.

ASPARAGUS WITH MINT & FETA

BRAISED CHICKEN WITH BROAD BEANS & LEEK

SPRING FRUIT SALAD

More chardonnay—this time, try an unwooded style like Plantagenet's Omrah Unoaked Chardonnay from sunny Western Australia or Chapel Hill's Unwooded Chardonnay from McLaren Vale in South Australia

BUDGET-FRIENDLY

This menu brings the best of spring to your table at an affordable price. For a wonderful variation on the asparagus with mint & feta, use soft goat's cheese instead of feta. It is a little more expensive, but it's worth it.

ASPARAGUS WITH MINT & FETA

serves: 6   prep: 10 mins   cooking: 5 mins

3   bunches (about 30 spears) asparagus, trimmed
90g   feta, crumbled

dressing
1½ tbs   olive oil
1 tbs   fresh lemon juice
½ tsp   Dijon mustard
2 tbs   shredded fresh mint
   Pinch of sugar
   Salt & ground black pepper, to taste

1   Bring a deep frying pan of water to the boil. Add the asparagus and cook, uncovered, for 1 minute or until bright green and tender crisp. (See microwave tip.) Drain and place in a large bowl of iced water to refresh. Drain well.

2   To make the dressing, place the oil, lemon juice, mustard, mint and sugar in a screw-top jar and shake well to combine. Season with salt and pepper.

3   Place the asparagus on a serving platter or individual plates and pour the dressing over. Sprinkle with the feta, and serve.

microwave tip: wash the asparagus and place in a freezer bag, adjusting until they are 2–3 deep when the bag is laid flat. Twist the opening to secure. Cook on High/800watts/100% for 3–4 minutes or until bright green and tender crisp.

BRAISED CHICKEN WITH BROAD BEANS & LEEK

serves: 6   prep: 15 mins   cooking: 45 mins

2 tbs	plain flour
	Salt & ground black pepper
6	(about 1.4kg) chicken thigh pieces
2 tbs	olive oil
3	leeks, white part only, cut into 5cm lengths
4	large garlic cloves, crushed
500ml	(2 cups) chicken or vegetable stock
375ml	(1½ cups) dry white wine
8	fresh thyme sprigs
2	bay leaves
185ml	(¾ cup) thin cream
500g	frozen broad beans, thawed, peeled
375ml	(1½ cups) water
380g	(2 cups) couscous

1 Place flour on a large plate and season with salt and pepper. Toss the chicken thighs in flour to coat. Heat 1 tbs oil in a large heavy-based saucepan over medium-high heat. Add half the chicken and cook, turning often, for 5 minutes or until golden. Transfer to a plate lined with paper towel and cover. Repeat with remaining chicken thighs.

2 Wipe out pan with paper towel. Add remaining 1 tbs oil and heat over medium heat. Add leeks and cook, stirring often, for 5 minutes or until they soften. Add garlic and stir for 1 minute or until aromatic.

3 Add 375ml (1½ cups) of stock to the pan with the wine, thyme and bay leaves. Stir, then cover, increase heat to high and bring to the boil. Reduce heat to medium and add the chicken. Cover and cook for 10–15 minutes or until the chicken is cooked through.

4 Transfer chicken to a plate and cover to keep warm. Add cream to the pan and stir well. Simmer, uncovered, over medium-high heat for 10 minutes. Stir in broad beans and simmer for a further 5 minutes or until beans are tender and sauce thickens slightly. Stir in the chicken.

5 Meanwhile, place the remaining stock and the water in a medium saucepan. Cover and bring to the boil over high heat. Remove from the heat and use a fork to stir in the couscous. Cover and set aside for 3–5 minutes, then use the fork to separate the grains. Serve the couscous with the chicken, vegetables and sauce.

variation: CHICKEN WITH BROAD BEANS & HERB MASH
Omit the couscous. Place 1.5kg sebago (brushed) potatoes, peeled, cut into 3cm chunks, in a large saucepan.
Cover with cold water and bring to the boil over high heat. Boil for 15 minutes or until soft. Drain and set aside for 5 minutes.
Return the potatoes to the pan, add 80g butter and use a potato masher to mash until smooth. Stir in 125ml (½ cup) warmed milk, ⅓ cup chopped fresh continental parsley, ½ cup chopped fresh chives, salt and ground black pepper. Serve immediately with chicken, vegetables and sauce.

SPRING FRUIT SALAD

serves: 6   prep: 10 mins (+ 15 mins standing time)

Did you know that rockmelons don't ripen further once they are picked? When buying one, smell it and make sure it has an intense, fresh aroma—a sure sign of ripeness. It should also feel heavy for its size.

500g (2 punnets) strawberries, hulled, halved

4 oranges, peeled, segmented

½ ripe rockmelon, peeled, cut into thin wedges

2 tbs caster sugar

200g natural yoghurt

1 tbs icing sugar, sifted

1   Place the strawberries, oranges, rockmelon and sugar in a large bowl. Toss well to combine. Set aside for 15 minutes.

2   Meanwhile, combine yoghurt and icing sugar in a small bowl.

3   Divide the fruit salad among serving plates or bowls. Drizzle the salad with any juices and top with a dollop of sweetened yoghurt.

variation: RUBY GRAPEFRUIT & STRAWBERRY SALAD

Replace the oranges with 3 ruby grapefruit, segmented. Add the pulp from 2 passionfruit to the sweetened yoghurt.

autumn menu for four

QUICK THAI FISHCAKES

RED PORK CURRY
WITH EGGPLANT & BASIL

STIR-FRIED CHOY SUM

STEAMED JASMINE RICE

PAWPAW & BANANA
WITH SWEET ORANGE SYRUP

A spicy, aromatic white—a gewürztraminer from Knappstein or Delatite would make an ideal partner

TANTALISING THAI

This menu is so easy, you'll never order take-away again! Thai food is renowned for its bold flavour combinations that balance hot, sweet, salty and sour. These dishes aren't strictly traditional but they do recognise this quality. A table-setting tip—Thais traditionally use a spoon and fork, rather than chopsticks.

QUICK THAI FISHCAKES

serves: 4   prep: 15 mins (+ 30 mins cooling time)   cooking: 10 mins

Process the fishcake ingredients until they are only just combined to ensure their texture is light. Seasoned rice wine vinegar is available from selected supermarkets and Asian food stores.

300g boneless white fish fillets (like flake or ling), cut into 2cm pieces

3 green shallots, trimmed, thinly sliced

½ bunch coriander, roughly chopped

1 garlic clove, finely chopped

3cm piece fresh ginger, finely grated

1 lemon grass stem, pale section only, finely chopped

1 tsp fish sauce

Vegetable oil, for frying

dipping sauce

60ml (¼ cup) water

60ml (¼ cup) seasoned rice wine vinegar

2 tbs caster sugar

1 small fresh red chilli, deseeded, finely chopped

¼ Lebanese cucumber, deseeded, finely diced

2 tbs chopped unsalted roasted peanuts

1 To make the dipping sauce, place the water, vinegar and sugar in a small saucepan. Stir over low heat until the sugar dissolves. Increase heat to high and simmer for 2 minutes. (See microwave tip.) Remove from the heat and set aside for 30 minutes to cool. Add the chilli, cucumber and peanuts, and set aside for a further 5 minutes for the flavours to infuse.

2 Meanwhile, combine the fish, green shallots, coriander, garlic, ginger, lemon grass and fish sauce in the bowl of a food processor. Process using the pulse button until just combined.

3 Use wet hands to shape the fish mixture into 12 even patties, each about 1cm thick.

4 Add enough oil to a large non-stick frying pan to reach 1cm up the side, and heat over medium heat. Add half the patties and cook for 1–1½ minutes each side or until golden and just cooked through. Transfer to paper towel to drain and cover with foil to keep warm. Repeat with the remaining patties. Serve the fishcakes warm with the dipping sauce.

microwave tip: place the water, vinegar and sugar in a small, heatproof microwave-safe jug or bowl. Heat, uncovered, on High/800watts/100% for 2 minutes, then stir until the sugar dissolves.

RED PORK CURRY WITH EGGPLANT & BASIL

serves: 4   prep: 20 mins   cooking: 20–25 mins

The quantity of curry paste used in this recipe will produce a curry with moderate heat. You can adjust the quantity of curry paste to suit your preferences. Thai (or holy) basil can be used instead of regular basil. It has a stronger flavour, purple-tinged stems and pointed leaves.

1	140ml can coconut cream
1½ tbs	Thai red curry paste, or to taste
3	small (about 180g) baby eggplant, thickly sliced
1	small carrot, peeled, thinly sliced
1	270ml can coconut milk
160ml	(²/³ cup) chicken stock
300g	pork fillet, thinly sliced
2 tbs	fish sauce
3 tsp	brown sugar
2	long fresh red chillies, thinly diagonally sliced
4	kaffir lime leaves, crushed
2 tbs	fresh lime juice
20	small fresh basil leaves

1   Place the coconut cream in a wok or frying pan and cook over medium heat, uncovered, stirring constantly, for 5 minutes or until it separates. Add the curry paste and cook, stirring constantly, for 1 minute or until aromatic.

2   Add the eggplant and carrot, and stir to coat in the coconut cream mixture. Stir in the coconut milk and stock, increase heat to high and bring to the boil. Reduce heat to low and simmer, uncovered, for 5 minutes.

3   Add the pork, fish sauce, sugar, chillies and lime leaves to the pan. Increase heat to high and return to the boil. Reduce heat to low and simmer, uncovered, for 3 minutes or until the pork is just cooked and the vegetables are tender. Remove from the heat and stir in the lime juice and basil leaves. Serve immediately.

STIR-FRIED CHOY SUM

serves: 4   prep: 5 mins   cooking: 3–5 mins

1 tbs	peanut oil
1	bunch choy sum, trimmed, washed, dried
2 tbs	oyster sauce
1 tsp	fish sauce

1   Heat the oil in a wok over high heat until smoking. Add the choy sum and stir-fry for 1–2 minutes or until it begins to wilt.

2   Add the oyster and fish sauces, and toss well. Cook for 1–2 minutes or until the choy sum is bright green. Serve immediately.

STEAMED JASMINE RICE

serves: 4   prep: 1 min (+ 10 mins standing time)   cooking: 20–25 mins

625ml	(2½ cups) water
300g	(1½ cups) jasmine rice

1   Bring the water to the boil in a medium heavy-based saucepan over high heat.

2   Add the rice, stir well and return to the boil. Reduce heat to very low, cover with a tight-fitting lid and cook gently for 15–20 minutes or until the water is absorbed and the rice is tender.

3   Remove the pan from the heat and set aside, covered, for 10 minutes. Use a fork to separate the grains, and serve.

PAWPAW & BANANA WITH SWEET ORANGE SYRUP

serves: 4 prep: 15 mins cooking: 20 mins

A ripe pawpaw will yield to gentle pressure at the stem end, and should be stored at room temperature until it reaches this stage.
Once ripe, it will keep in the fridge for up to 4 days.

250ml (1 cup) fresh orange juice (about 4 oranges)

110g (½ cup) caster sugar

1 large (about 1kg) pawpaw

2 ripe bananas

1 Place the orange juice and sugar in a small saucepan and stir over high heat until the sugar dissolves. Bring to the boil, then reduce heat to medium-low and simmer, uncovered, for 15 minutes or until the syrup thickens slightly. (See microwave tip.) Remove from the heat and set aside to cool while preparing the fruit.

2 Halve, deseed and peel the pawpaw. Quarter lengthways and then cut into 1cm-thick wedges. Peel the bananas and thickly diagonally slice. Combine the fruit and then divide among serving bowls. Spoon the orange syrup over, and serve.

microwave tip: place the orange juice and sugar in a 1-litre (4-cup), heatproof microwave-safe jug or bowl.
Cook, uncovered, on High/800watts/100%, stirring every minute, for 5–6 minutes or until the syrup thickens slightly.

SICILIAN STYLE

On a recent trip to Sicily I discovered the delights of this regional cuisine. Freshness is paramount, and flavours are combined in unusual yet harmonious ways. Above all, food is enjoyed—meals are noisy affairs, filled with laughter and a strong sense of family. This menu celebrates Sicilian flavours in an Australian setting.

WHITE BEAN & FENNEL SOUP

serves: 6   prep: 25 mins (+ overnight soaking time)   cooking: 2 hours

305g (1½ cups) dried great northern or
330g (1½ cups) cannellini beans
60ml (¼ cup) extra virgin olive oil
2 brown onions, finely chopped
6 drained anchovy fillets, chopped
3 garlic cloves, finely chopped
500g (about 4) baby fennel bulbs, fronds reserved
500g desiree potatoes, peeled, chopped
1L (4 cups) vegetable stock
1L (4 cups) water
Salt & ground black pepper, to taste
Extra virgin olive oil, extra, to serve
Crusty Italian bread, to serve

1 Place beans in a large bowl and cover with plenty of cold water. Cover and set aside overnight to soak. Drain and rinse, then drain again.

2 Heat the oil in a large, deep saucepan over medium heat. Add the onions, anchovies and garlic, and cook, stirring often, for 5 minutes or until the anchovies begin to break down. Cover and cook, stirring occasionally, for a further 5 minutes or until the onions are soft.

3 Remove tough outer layer from fennel and thinly slice lengthways. Add fennel and potatoes to the pan, and stir well. Cover and cook, stirring occasionally, for 10 minutes or until fennel softens slightly.

4 Add the drained beans, stock and water to the pan, and stir to combine. Increase heat to high, cover and bring to the boil. Reduce heat to medium and simmer, partially covered, stirring occasionally, for 45 minutes. Uncover and cook, stirring occasionally, for a further 30 minutes or until the beans are tender and the soup thickens slightly. Taste and season with salt and pepper.

5 Ladle the soup into serving bowls. Garnish with the reserved fennel fronds, and drizzle with a little extra virgin olive oil. Serve with the crusty bread.

CHARGRILLED SWORDFISH WITH OLIVE & CAPER SALSA

serves: 6   prep: 20 mins (+ 2 hours standing time)   cooking: 12–15 mins

6 (about 200g each) swordfish steaks
1 tbs extra virgin olive oil
  Salt & ground black pepper, to taste

olive & caper salsa

2 small lemons
135g (³/₄ cup) green olives, pitted, quartered
135g (³/₄ cup) kalamata olives, pitted, quartered
1 200g jar capers, drained,
  patted dry with paper towel
1 bunch continental parsley, leaves picked,
  roughly chopped
80ml (¹/₃ cup) extra virgin olive oil
  Ground black pepper, to taste

1 To make the salsa, use a zester to remove the rind from the lemons. (Alternatively, use a vegetable peeler to peel the rind from the lemons. Use a small sharp knife to remove the white pith from the rind. Cut the rind into very thin strips.) Juice the lemons. Place the lemon rind, lemon juice, olives, capers, parsley and oil in a medium bowl, and toss well to combine. Taste and season with pepper. Cover and set aside for 2 hours to allow the flavours to develop.

2 When ready to serve, heat a chargrill or large heavy-based frying pan over high heat. Brush both sides of the swordfish with oil and season lightly with salt and pepper. Add 3 steaks to the chargrill and reduce heat to medium-high. Cook for 3 minutes each side for medium or until cooked to your liking. Transfer to a warmed plate and cover loosely with foil to keep warm. Repeat with remaining steaks.

3 Serve the swordfish steaks immediately with the salsa.

BEANS WITH ANCHOVY GARLIC BREADCRUMBS

serves: 6   prep: 15 mins   cooking: 10–15 mins

Cooking the anchovies in oil until they begin to break down and disintegrate makes them less pungent, more mellow and slightly sweet—a perfect partner for freshly cooked beans.

80ml (¹/₃ cup) extra virgin olive oil
40g (about 14) drained anchovy fillets, roughly chopped
3 garlic cloves, cut into thin strips
600g green beans, topped
75g (1½ cups) fine breadcrumbs, made
  from day-old, Italian-style bread
  Ground black pepper, to taste

1 Heat oil in a large heavy-based frying pan over medium heat. Add the anchovies and garlic, and cook, stirring often, for 4–5 minutes or until anchovies begin to break down and garlic is golden. Remove from heat.

2 Meanwhile, steam the beans in a steaming basket over a saucepan of simmering water for 4–5 minutes or until they are bright green and tender crisp. (Alternatively, cook in boiling water.)

3 Transfer the beans to a heatproof bowl and add 1 tbs of the anchovy oil mixture. Toss well, cover to keep warm and set aside.

4 Heat the remaining anchovy oil mixture in the pan over medium-high heat. Add the breadcrumbs and cook, stirring, for 4–5 minutes or until they are crisp and golden brown. Season with pepper.

5 Place the beans on a serving platter and sprinkle with half the breadcrumb mixture. Place the remaining breadcrumb mixture in a small serving bowl to pass around separately.

ORANGE RICOTTA DESSERTS

serves: 6   prep: 30 mins (+ overnight draining, 30 mins setting and 4 hours chilling time)   cooking: 15–20 mins

This recipe can be made to the end of step 5 up to 1 day before serving. Macerate the oranges up to 4 hours ahead.

1kg fresh ricotta
6 oranges
400g (1¾ cups) caster sugar
80ml (⅓ cup) water
1½ tbs (30ml) dark rum
125ml (½ cup) thin cream
2 tbs caster sugar, extra

1   Line a large strainer with a double layer of muslin and place over a bowl. Place ricotta in the strainer and fold the muslin over to cover. Place a bowl on top of the ricotta with a few cans of food inside (this helps extract any excess moisture). Place in fridge overnight to drain.

2   Use a vegetable peeler to peel strips of rind from the oranges. Use a small sharp knife to remove white pith from rind. Cut the rind into 1cm-thick strips. Place the oranges in a bowl, cover and keep in the fridge. Line 2 large baking trays with non-stick baking paper.

3   Place 280g (1¼ cups) of sugar and the water in a large saucepan. Stir over low heat until sugar dissolves. Brush down saucepan with a wet pastry brush to remove any sugar crystals. Increase heat to high, add the rind and bring to the boil. Boil, uncovered, brushing down the side of the pan occasionally with the wet brush, for 10–15 minutes or until

the syrup is golden. Use a fork to quickly transfer the rind to the lined trays. Set the rind aside for 30 minutes or until set. Place a third of the candied rind in an airtight container lined with non-stick baking paper and set aside. Chop the remaining rind and place in a bowl.

4   Place the ricotta, remaining sugar and 2 tsp of the rum in the bowl of a food processor. Process, scraping down the side of the bowl occasionally, until smooth. Add the cream and process to combine. Add to the chopped rind and mix to combine.

5   Line six 185ml (¾-cup) dishes with plastic wrap, allowing it to hang over the sides. Divide mixture evenly among lined dishes and use the back of a spoon to press down and smooth the surface. Fold the overhanging plastic wrap over to cover completely. Place on a tray in the fridge for at least 4 hours to firm slightly.

6   Meanwhile, use a small sharp knife to cut the white pith from oranges. Cut the oranges into 1cm-thick rounds. Place a layer of orange rounds in a medium shallow dish. Sprinkle with a little each of the extra sugar and remaining rum. Repeat with the remaining oranges, sugar and rum. Cover and set aside for at least 1 hour to macerate.

7   To serve, use the plastic wrap to remove desserts from dishes. Turn onto serving plates and remove the plastic wrap. Top with the reserved rind and serve with the macerated oranges.

Celebrations come in all shapes and sizes—from birthday dinners to romantic wedding banquets, from Christmas gatherings to smart cocktail parties. And each requires its own special festive menu. The menus that follow are the kind that make celebrations truly memorable.

The recipes are impressive, yet simple and headache-free; the flavours fresh and inviting. It is food to entertain a crowd. I have not given season suggestions for these menus, because most celebrations can't be moved around the calendar to suit!

SMOKED SALMON
WITH DILL MAYONNAISE

CRUSTY BREAD

SPATCHCOCK WITH
LIME & MUSTARD BASTE

BEANS WITH
RED WINE VINAIGRETTE

POTATOES WITH PERSILLADE

LEMON CREAM CAKE

I can see several bottles of delicious pinot noir being the perfect birthday present—it's hard to go past Coldstream Hills or Yering Station, both from the Yarra Valley in Victoria

BIRTHDAY

Whatever the age, there is no better excuse for a celebration than a birthday. It is a time to fuss and pamper, to make a person feel extra special. This meal needs only friends and family—and a few bottles of good wine. Start with smoked salmon, follow up with succulent spatchcock and finish with a truly luscious lemon birthday cake. A year seems far too long to wait for a repeat performance of this star menu!

SMOKED SALMON WITH DILL MAYONNAISE

picture page 139

serves: 8 prep: 25 mins

This quantity of mayonnaise is quite small, so you may need to tilt the food processor when making it to allow the mixture to cover the blade. The mayonnaise will store in the fridge for up to 1 week.

160g baby spinach leaves, trimmed, washed, dried

800g sliced smoked salmon

Salt & ground black pepper, to taste

2 lemons, cut into wedges

Crusty bread, to serve

dill mayonnaise

2 egg yolks

1 tbs fresh lemon juice

100ml olive oil

1 tbs drained capers, finely chopped

1 tbs roughly chopped fresh dill leaves

½ tsp Tabasco sauce

1 tbs water

Salt & ground black pepper, to taste

1 To make the mayonnaise, place the egg yolks and lemon juice in the bowl of a food processor and process to combine. With the motor running, gradually add the oil in a thin, steady stream until the mayonnaise thickens. Transfer to a bowl. Stir in the capers, dill, Tabasco and water. Taste and season with salt and pepper.

2 Place the baby spinach leaves on a large serving plate. Arrange the smoked salmon on the spinach and sprinkle with salt and pepper.

3 Serve with the mayonnaise, lemon wedges and crusty bread.

SPATCHCOCK WITH LIME & MUSTARD BASTE

serves: 8 prep: 15 mins (+ 15 mins resting time) cooking: 30 mins

4 (600–700g each) fresh spatchcock or poussin

Salt & ground black pepper, to taste

lime & mustard baste

90ml (4½ tbs) fresh lime juice

60ml (¼ cup) olive oil

60g (3 tbs) butter, cubed

1½ tbs Dijon mustard

1 Preheat oven to 200°C. Line a large baking tray with non-stick baking paper.

2 To make the baste, place the lime juice, oil and butter in a small saucepan over medium heat. Stir for 2–3 minutes or until the butter melts. (See microwave tip.) Add the mustard and whisk well to combine. Set aside.

3 Use sharp kitchen scissors to cut the spatchcock in half lengthways. Place the spatchcock halves, cut-side down, on the lined tray.

4 Brush the spatchcock generously with the baste and season with salt and pepper. Roast in preheated oven, brushing with remaining baste halfway through cooking, for 30 minutes or until golden and juices run clear when pierced in the thickest part of the thigh with a skewer.

5 Cover loosely with foil and set aside in a warm place for 15 minutes to rest before serving.

BEANS WITH RED WINE VINAIGRETTE

serves: 8 prep: 10 mins cooking: 5 mins

400g green beans, topped

400g butter (yellow) beans, topped

red wine vinaigrette

60ml (¼ cup) olive oil

2 tbs red wine vinegar

1 tsp caster sugar

1 tsp wholegrain mustard

Salt & ground black pepper, to taste

1 Cook the beans in a medium saucepan of salted boiling water for 2–3 minutes or until tender crisp. Drain and return to the pan.

2 Meanwhile, to make the vinaigrette, place the oil, vinegar, sugar, mustard, salt and pepper in a small screw-top jar, and shake well to combine.

3 Pour the vinaigrette over the warm beans and toss well to combine. Serve immediately.

POTATOES WITH PERSILLADE

picture page 141

serves: 8   prep: 15 mins (+ 30 mins cooling time)   cooking: 55-65 mins

1.4kg   (about 8) desiree potatoes, scrubbed
25g   (5 tsp) butter, chopped
60ml   (¼ cup) olive oil
800g   orange sweet potato (kumara), peeled
⅓ cup   chopped fresh continental parsley
4   garlic cloves, finely chopped
Salt & ground black pepper, to taste

1   Preheat oven to 200°C. Cut half the potatoes into 1cm-thick slices.

2   Heat the butter and half the oil in a roasting pan over medium-high heat. Add the sliced potatoes and reduce heat to medium. Cook, uncovered, for 5 minutes each side or until golden. Transfer to a plate and set aside. Repeat with the remaining potatoes and then the sweet potato, in one batch each, adding a little of the remaining oil if necessary.

3   Return the potato and sweet potato slices to the roasting pan. Cook in preheated oven for 15 minutes or until tender and heated through.

4   Meanwhile, combine the parsley and garlic in a small bowl.

5   Place the potato and sweet potato slices on serving plates. Sprinkle with the parsley and garlic mixture, then season with salt and pepper. Serve immediately.

LEMON CREAM CAKE

serves: 8   prep: 25 mins (+ 30 mins cooling and 1 hour setting time)   cooking: 35 mins
Make the filling and glaze for this cake just before you assemble it.

Melted butter, for greasing
5   eggs, at room temperature
400g   (1¾ cups) caster sugar
450g   (3 cups) plain flour
3 tsp   baking powder
500ml   (2 cups) thickened cream
3   lemons, rind finely grated, juiced
2   lemons, extra, to decorate

cream filling
250ml   (1 cup) thickened cream
60g   (⅓ cup) icing sugar, sifted

lemon glaze
300g   (2 cups) pure icing sugar, sifted
60ml   (¼ cup) strained fresh lemon juice

1   Preheat oven to 180°C. Brush 2 round 22cm cake pans with the melted butter to grease, then line the base and side of each with non-stick baking paper.

2   Use electric beaters to whisk the eggs and sugar in a large bowl until a ribbon trail forms when the beaters are lifted.

3   Sift the flour and baking powder together. Combine the cream, lemon rind and 60ml (¼ cup) of lemon juice. Use a large metal spoon or spatula to gently fold half the flour mixture into egg mixture. Fold in the cream mixture, then remaining flour mixture until just combined.

4   Divide the cake mixture between the prepared pans and smooth the surface of each. Bake in preheated oven for 35 minutes or until light golden and a skewer inserted in the centres of the cakes comes out clean. Set aside for 5 minutes before turning onto wire racks to cool.

5   To make the filling, use electric beaters or a balloon whisk to whisk the cream and icing sugar in a medium bowl until soft peaks form.

6   To make the glaze, place icing sugar in a medium bowl and make a well in the centre. Add the lemon juice and use a wooden spoon to gradually incorporate the icing sugar to form a thin paste. Transfer to a jug.

7   To assemble the cake, place a cake layer on a wire rack over a tray. Spread the filling over the top, then cover with remaining cake layer. Gradually pour icing on centre of top cake layer, so it drips unevenly down the side. Set aside in a cool place for 1 hour or until icing sets.

8   Meanwhile, use a zester to remove rind from lemons. (Alternatively, use a vegetable peeler to remove the rind. Use a small sharp knife to remove any white pith from the rind, then cut the rind into very thin strips.) Place in an airtight container in the fridge until required. Decorate the cake with the strips of lemon rind just before serving.

BAKED FETA

CRUSTY BREAD

ROAST LAMB WITH
LEMON & GARLIC

ROAST POTATOES & CELERIAC
WITH EGG & LEMON SAUCE

MIXED GREEN SALAD

BAKLAVA POUCHES

---

*Coonawarra cabernet sauvignon is the
perfect partner for roast lamb—try
Robertson's Well or Bowen Estate*

EASTER SUNDAY

*These recipes are from an Australian friend of
Greek descent. They're inspired by the flavours
and ingredients typically associated with Greek
food, such as feta, lamb, honey, figs, lemons,
green olives, olive oil, garlic, rosemary, oregano
and cinnamon. This menu is a modern take
on traditional Greek food eaten over Easter.
An intriguing meal to share and celebrate.*

BAKED FETA

serves: 8   prep: 10 mins   cooking: 10 mins

1   large loaf crusty bread, unsliced
1   450g piece Greek feta, halved horizontally
80ml (⅓ cup) extra virgin olive oil
½ tsp   sweet paprika
½ tsp   dried oregano
½ tsp   freshly ground black pepper

1   Preheat oven to 200°C. Cut the bread into 2cm-thick slices.
Reassemble the loaf, then wrap in foil and place on a baking tray.

2   Place the feta in two 4cm-deep, round 14cm ovenproof dishes.
Combine the oil, paprika, oregano and pepper in a small jug and
pour evenly over the feta.

3   Place the feta and bread in preheated oven and bake for 10 minutes
or until heated through and the feta softens slightly. Serve the feta
immediately straight from the dishes with the warm bread.

ROAST LAMB WITH LEMON & GARLIC

picture page 147

serves: 8   prep: 20 mins (+ 10 mins resting time)   cooking: 1 hour 25 mins

*You can use two 1.25kg Easy Carve legs of lamb in this recipe—cook for only 50 minutes when the temperature is reduced to 180°C. The pan
juices can be used in the egg & lemon sauce (recipe page 146), if you like. While the lamb is resting, carefully pour the juices into a medium
heatproof jug. Skim the top layer of fat from the surface, measure 125ml (½ cup) and add 125ml (½ cup) water. Use instead of the chicken stock.*

1   lemon, halved
1½ tsp   dried oregano
1½ tsp   salt
1½ tsp   ground black pepper
2   1.8kg legs of lamb
7   small garlic cloves, cut into thick slices
6   fresh rosemary sprigs

1   Preheat oven to 240°C.

2   Juice the lemon halves and reserve the juice. Cut each juiced lemon
half into quarters to make 8 pieces of lemon rind. Set aside. Combine
the oregano, salt and pepper in a small bowl and set aside. ·

3   Use a small sharp knife to make small incisions all over each leg of
lamb and insert the slices of garlic. Spread the lemon rind pieces over
the base of a large non-aluminium roasting pan and place the legs of
lamb on top. Rub each leg of lamb all over with the oregano mixture.
Pour half the lemon juice over the legs of lamb.

4   Roast in preheated oven for 20 minutes. Reduce oven temperature to
180°C. Place 3 sprigs of rosemary on each leg of lamb and cover the
pan with a lid or foil. Roast for a further 1 hour 5 minutes for
medium or until cooked to your liking.

5   Transfer the lamb to 2 large plates, cover loosely with foil and set
aside in a warm place for 10 minutes to rest. Carve the lamb and
serve warm, drizzled with some of the pan juices.

MIXED GREEN SALAD

serves: 8   prep: 10 mins

2 medium bunches cos lettuce
120g baby rocket leaves, washed, dried
4 green shallots, trimmed, chopped
2 tbs chopped fresh dill leaves
2 tbs chopped fresh continental parsley leaves
200g drained marinated green olives

dressing
80ml (⅓ cup) extra virgin olive oil
2 tbs fresh lemon juice
Salt & ground black pepper, to taste

1 Remove the coarse outer leaves from the cos lettuce and discard. Separate the remaining leaves and wash well. Drain well. Shred into 1cm-thick strips and place in a large bowl. Add the rocket, green shallots, dill and parsley, and toss to combine. Cover and place in the fridge for up to 2 hours before serving.

2 To make the dressing, use a fork to whisk the oil, lemon juice, salt and pepper in a small jug until well combined.

3 Just before serving, pour the dressing over the salad and toss well. Place in 1 large or 2 small serving bowls and sprinkle with the olives.

ROAST POTATOES & CELERIAC WITH EGG & LEMON SAUCE

serves: 8   prep: 20 mins   cooking: 1 hour 10 mins
If serving these vegetables with the roast lamb with lemon & garlic (recipe page 144), place the legs of lamb in 2 separate roasting pans and arrange the vegetables around them.

1 lemon, halved
1.2kg desiree or King Edward potatoes, scrubbed
1.2kg celeriac
60g (3 tbs) butter, melted
Salt & ground black pepper, to taste

egg & lemon sauce
250ml (1 cup) chicken stock
125ml (½ cup) water
15g (3 tsp) butter
2 tsp plain flour
2 eggs
1 tbs fresh lemon juice
2 tsp fresh thyme leaves
Salt & ground black pepper, to taste

1 Preheat oven to 240°C.

2 Juice the lemon halves and reserve the juice. Cut each juiced lemon half into quarters to make 8 pieces of lemon rind.

3 Cut the potatoes into 4–5cm chunks and place in a large bowl. Trim the celeriac, peel and cut into 4–5 cm chunks. Add to the potatoes with the pieces of lemon rind, lemon juice, butter, salt and pepper. Use your hands to toss the vegetables to coat.

4 Place the vegetables in 2 non-aluminium roasting pans. Roast in preheated oven for 20 minutes. Reduce oven temperature to 180°C. Cover the pans with lids or foil and bake for a further 50 minutes or until the vegetables are tender.

5 Combine the stock and water in a jug. Melt the butter in a medium saucepan over high heat. Add the flour and use a whisk to stir constantly until bubbling. Remove from the heat and gradually stir in half the stock mixture until smooth. Stir in the remaining stock mixture and return the pan to high heat. Continue stirring until the sauce boils and thickens, then reduce heat to medium and simmer, uncovered, stirring occasionally, for 2 minutes. Remove from the heat.

6 Use a clean whisk to whisk the eggs and lemon juice in a medium bowl until frothy. Continue to whisk while gradually adding about 125ml (½ cup) of the hot sauce. Pour the egg mixture into the pan containing the remaining sauce and stir over low heat until the sauce thickens slightly (the froth will disappear). Don't let the sauce simmer. Stir in the thyme. Taste and season with salt and pepper, if necessary.

7 Place the vegetables in a large serving dish and pour over some of the sauce. Serve the remaining sauce separately.

BAKLAVA POUCHES

serves: 8   prep: 40 mins (+ 2 hours cooling time)   cooking: 1¼ hours

These more-ish pouches can be made to the end of step 6 up to 3 days ahead. Store in an airtight container in a cool place (but not in the fridge or the filo will soften). They are best served on the day the syrup is poured over.

50g (2½ tbs) cultured unsalted butter, melted
      Pinch of salt
60g (⅓ cup) almonds
35g (⅓ cup) good-quality walnut halves
75g (¼ cup) dried dessert figs, finely chopped
1 tsp ground cinnamon
¼ tsp ground cloves
1 tbs caster sugar
3 sheets filo pastry

syrup
125ml (½ cup) water
220g (1 cup) caster sugar
3 (about 8cm long) orange rind strips
1 tbs fresh orange juice
2 tbs honey

1 Preheat oven to 160°C. Combine the melted butter and salt. Brush a baking tray with a little of the salted butter to grease.

2 Place half each of the almonds and walnuts in the bowl of a food processor and use the pulse button to process until finely chopped, but not powdery. Transfer to a medium bowl and repeat with the remaining almonds and walnuts. Add the figs, cinnamon, cloves and sugar, and use your hands to mix until well combined.

3 Place the filo pastry on a work surface. Cover with a clean tea towel and then a damp tea towel (this will help prevent it drying out). Brush a sheet of filo with a little salted butter. Top with another sheet of filo and brush with a little more salted butter. Continue to layer with the remaining filo and salted butter.

4 Cut the layered filo in half to form 2 pieces, then cut each half into 4 smaller squares. Divide the nut mixture among the centres of the squares. Gather the edges of a filo square together and gently press to form a pouch (the pouches don't need to close completely). Place on the greased tray. Repeat with the remaining filo squares.

5 Bake in preheated oven for 1 hour or until the filo is golden brown and crisp. (You can cover the pouches loosely with brown paper after 30 minutes if the tops are browning too quickly.)

6 Remove from the oven and set aside on the tray for 1 hour or until cooled completely.

7 Meanwhile, to make the syrup, place the water, sugar, orange rind strips and orange juice in a medium saucepan. Stir over low heat until the sugar dissolves. Use a wet pastry brush to brush down the side of the pan to remove any sugar crystals. Bring to the boil, reduce heat to medium and simmer, uncovered, without stirring, for 5 minutes or until syrup thickens slightly. Remove from heat and add the honey. Return to high heat and bring to the boil, then remove from the heat. (See microwave tip.) Pour the hot syrup over the pouches and serve warm or at room temperature.

microwave tip: place water, sugar, orange rind strips and orange juice in a medium, heatproof microwave-safe jug or bowl. Heat on High/800watts/100%, stirring every minute, for 2–3 minutes or until sugar dissolves. Use a wet pastry brush to brush side of jug to remove sugar crystals. Cook on Medium/500watts/50% for a further 3–5 minutes or until syrup thickens slightly. Stir in honey and heat on High/800watts/100% for 1 minute.

You must have a couple of bottles of lovely bubbles at a christening and it's hard to go past Domaine Chandon, the Aussie version of Moët & Chandon, or Jansz from Tasmania

CHRISTENING

Everyone loves a tea party—especially when it involves children. A morning or afternoon tea is a lovely way to celebrate a christening or other special family occasion.

Stacking the cupcakes was an idea that I originally used as a first birthday cake for my daughter, Brooke. It was a huge success— easy to prepare and even easier to serve! This menu is sure to charm and delight.

PASSIONFRUIT CUPCAKES

makes: 42   prep: 20 mins (+ 30 mins cooling time)   cooking: 20–24 mins

You will need about 5 passionfruit. The cupcakes can be made up to 1 day ahead—keep them in an airtight container. You can stack the cupcakes as we have done to form a pretty and very effective celebration cake. We used bouvardia flowers to decorate.

Melted butter, for greasing
200g butter, at room temperature
220g (1 cup) caster sugar
1 tsp vanilla essence
3 eggs, at room temperature
125ml (½ cup) passionfruit pulp
300g (2 cups) self-raising flour, sifted
Icing sugar, to dust
Flowers of your choice, to decorate

1 Preheat oven to 180°C. Brush 24 mini (30ml/1½ tbs) muffin pans with the melted butter to grease.

2 Use electric beaters to beat the butter, sugar and vanilla essence in a medium bowl until very pale and creamy. Add the eggs one at a time, beating well after each addition. Use a large metal spoon to stir in the passionfruit pulp until combined. Fold in flour until just combined.

3 Spoon half the cake mixture into the greased pans, dividing it evenly among them. Bake in preheated oven for 10–12 minutes or until light golden and a skewer inserted in the centres of the cakes comes out clean. Remove from the oven and set aside for 5 minutes before turning onto a wire rack to cool completely. Brush the muffin pans again with melted butter to grease and repeat with the remaining cake mixture (you will have enough mixture for 18 more cupcakes).

4 To assemble, place 18 cupcakes on a serving plate to form a circle. Top with 14 of the remaining cupcakes. Continue to layer with 7 cupcakes in the third layer and then 3 in the fourth. Dust the cupcakes generously with the icing sugar and then decorate with the flowers, as desired.

ARTICHOKE PUREE SERVED WITH ASPARAGUS, BEANS & CUCUMBER

serves: 20 (makes about 750ml/3 cups puree)   prep: 20 mins   cooking: 10 mins

The puree can be made up to 1 day ahead. You can prepare and cook the vegetables up to 4 hours before serving.
Keep the puree and vegetables in separate airtight containers in the fridge.

3 bunches (about 30 stems) asparagus, ends trimmed

350g green beans, topped

6 Lebanese cucumbers, cut into sticks

artichoke puree

2 340g jars marinated artichoke hearts, drained (125ml/½ cup liquid reserved)

80ml (⅓ cup) double cream

Salt & ground black pepper, to taste

1 To make artichoke puree, place artichokes and reserved liquid in the bowl of a food processor. Process until smooth. Transfer to a bowl, add cream, salt and pepper, and mix well. Cover and place in fridge.

2 Bring a large saucepan of salted water to the boil. Add half the asparagus and cook for 2 minutes or until bright green. Use a slotted spoon to transfer the asparagus to a bowl of iced water to refresh until cold. Drain well. Return the water to the boil and repeat with the remaining asparagus. (See microwave tip 1.)

3 Return water to the boil, add beans and cook for 1–2 minutes or until bright green. (See microwave tip 2.) Drain, refresh and drain again.

4 Spoon the puree into a serving bowl and place on a serving platter. Arrange asparagus, beans and cucumbers around the bowl, and serve.

microwave tip 1: wash the asparagus and place in a freezer bag, adjusting until they are 1–2 deep when the bag is laid flat. Twist the opening to secure. Cook on High/800watts/100% for 3–4 minutes or until bright green. Refresh in a bowl of iced water. Repeat with remaining asparagus.

microwave tip 2: wash beans and place in a freezer bag. Twist opening to secure. Cook for 2–3 minutes on High/800watts/100% or until bright green.

SELECTION OF SANDWICHES

Choose a variety of fillings from the following suggestions and make a total of 20 sandwiches. You can make them up to 6 hours before serving—wrap them well in plastic wrap, then a damp tea towel, and keep in the fridge until ready to serve.

- Smoked salmon slices topped with chopped capers & black pepper on white bread spread with sour cream.
- Thinly sliced ham on buttered white bread spread with wholegrain mustard.
- Thinly sliced cucumber topped with chopped chives & black pepper on white bread spread with sour cream.
- Mashed hard-boiled egg combined with mayonnaise & chopped parsley on buttered white bread.
- Chopped smoked chicken combined with chopped dill, mayonnaise & cranberry jelly on buttered brown bread.
- Grilled eggplant topped with rocket, salt and ground black pepper on brown bread spread with hummus.

To cut into triangles, place one sandwich on top of another and use a bread knife to remove the crusts from both. Turn the sandwich stack upside down (this will help keep the triangles the same size) and cut into 4 triangles.

TURKISH DELIGHT & NUT PASTRIES

makes: 30   prep: 40 mins (+ 15 mins cooling time)   cooking: 15 mins

These pastries will keep in an airtight container lined with baking paper for up to 4 days.

340g   Turkish delight, cut into 1cm pieces

85g   (½ cup) blanched almonds, finely chopped

75g   (½ cup) raw unsalted pistachio nuts, finely chopped

1 tsp   ground cinnamon

20   sheets (375g pkt) filo pastry

140g   butter, melted

2 tbs   honey

2 tbs   chopped raw unsalted pistachio nuts, extra

1   Preheat oven to 190°C. Line 2 large baking trays with non-stick baking paper.

2   Place the Turkish delight, almonds, pistachio nuts and cinnamon in a bowl and toss to combine.

3   Place the filo on a work surface. Cover with a clean tea towel and then a damp tea towel (this will help prevent it drying out). Brush a sheet of filo lightly with melted butter and then top with another sheet of filo. Cut crossways into 3 even strips. Brush the long sides of the pastry lightly with butter. Spoon about 1 tbs of Turkish delight mixture onto a narrow end of the filo strip, leaving a 2cm border on each side. Fold in the sides and then roll up firmly, brushing the end with butter to seal. Place, seam-side down, on a lined tray and brush lightly with butter. Repeat with the remaining filo, butter and Turkish delight mixture.

4   Bake the pastries in preheated oven, swapping the trays halfway through cooking, for 15 minutes or until light golden and crisp.

5   Meanwhile, place the honey in a small cup. Place the cup in a small bowl of hot water until honey is runny. (See microwave tip.) Use a pastry brush to brush the honey evenly over the hot pastries, then sprinkle with the extra pistachio nuts. Set aside for 15 minutes to cool slightly before serving warm, or cool to room temperature.

microwave tip: place the honey in a small, heatproof microwave-safe bowl or cup. Heat, uncovered, on High/800watts/100% for 30–45 seconds.

HONEY & CINNAMON HEARTS

makes: 70   prep: 20 mins (+ 30 mins chilling, cooling and 30 mins setting time)   cooking: 20 mins
These biscuits will keep in an airtight container, layered with baking paper, for up to 1 week.

125g   butter, chilled, cubed
80ml   (⅓ cup) honey
2 tbs   caster sugar
265g   (1¾ cups) self-raising flour
½ tsp   ground cinnamon

icing
150g   (1 cup) pure icing sugar
3½ tsp   boiling water

1   Place the butter, honey and sugar in the bowl of a food processor and process until well combined and pale. Sift the flour and cinnamon over the butter mixture. Process briefly, scraping down the side of the bowl when necessary, until the mixture just begins to come together.

2   Turn the mixture onto a lightly floured surface and bring together with your hands. Shape into a disc, wrap in plastic wrap and place in the fridge for 30 minutes to chill.

3   Preheat oven to 180°C. Line 2 baking trays with non-stick paper.

4   Use a lightly floured rolling pin to roll half the dough on a lightly floured surface until about 4mm thick. Use a heart-shaped cutter, 4cm across, or cutter of choice to cut out dough. Place on lined trays and bake in preheated oven, swapping trays halfway through cooking, for 10 minutes or until light golden and cooked through. Cool on the trays, then transfer to a wire rack. Repeat with the remaining dough.

5   To make the icing, sift the icing sugar into a bowl. Add the boiling water and stir until smooth. Spoon into a freezer bag and cut a small hole in one corner. Drizzle the biscuits with the icing to decorate. Set aside for about 30 minutes for the icing to set.

CITRUS & MINT TEA

makes: 1L (4 cups) prep: 5 mins (+ 5 mins infusing time)
You will need to make 3 times this quantity to serve 20.

1   lemon
5cm   piece fresh ginger, peeled, thinly sliced
5   large fresh mint sprigs
1L   (4 cups) boiling water
4   limes, halved, to serve
8   small squares of muslin
   Small fresh mint leaves, extra, to serve

1   Use a vegetable peeler to thinly peel 4 pieces of rind, about 6cm long, from lemons. Place lemon rind, ginger and mint in a large teapot or coffee plunger. Add boiling water and set aside for 5 minutes to infuse.

2   Meanwhile, wrap each lime half in a small square of muslin and tie with a small piece of string to secure.

3   Place the extra mint leaves in small teacups and pour the hot tea over. Serve with the lime halves, to add lime juice to taste.

menu for eight (for under $60)

INDIVIDUAL CHEESE & SPINACH TARTS

OSSO BUCCO

CREAMY POLENTA

SAUTEED ONION WITH PEAS

ORANGE ZABAGLIONE WITH STRAWBERRIES

Try a couple of the good-value Rosemount wines. The Semillon Chardonnay and Shiraz Cabernet are always great

BUDGET-FRIENDLY

Italian cooking offers flavour without the fuss—it uses simple ingredients in basic ways to produce something not only memorable, but also quite economical. This menu uses these principles to transform rustic flavours into a fabulous feast.

INDIVIDUAL CHEESE & SPINACH TARTS

picture page 159

serves: 8   prep: 15 mins   cooking: 25–30 mins

40g (2 tbs) butter, melted

1 large bunch (about 280g) English spinach, trimmed

1 tbs olive oil

1 tsp ground or freshly grated nutmeg

3 eggs, lightly whisked

250g fresh ricotta

100g feta, crumbled

Ground black pepper, to taste

4 sheets filo pastry

1 Preheat oven to 190°C. Brush 8 large (250ml/1-cup) muffin pans with a little of the melted butter to lightly grease.

2 Wash, dry and shred the spinach. Heat oil in a large frying pan over medium heat. Add spinach and nutmeg, and cook for 2 minutes or until spinach just wilts and liquid evaporates. Place in a colander and set aside for 5 minutes to cool slightly. Squeeze out any excess liquid.

3 Place the eggs, ricotta and feta in a large bowl and mix well. Add the spinach, season well with pepper and mix to combine.

4 Working quickly, lay the filo sheets on top of each other on a work surface. Cut in half lengthways and then cut each strip into 4 even pieces. Cover the filo with a clean tea towel and then a damp tea towel (this will help prevent the filo drying out).

5 Brush 4 pieces of the filo with a little of the melted butter and layer unevenly in a greased pan, pressing into the base and side to fit. Repeat with the remaining pieces of filo and melted butter.

6 Spoon the spinach mixture evenly into the pastry cases. Bake in preheated oven for 20–25 minutes or until the filling is just set and the pastry is golden and crisp. Serve immediately.

OSSO BUCCO

serves: 8   prep: 15 mins   cooking: 2¼–2½ hours

50g (⅓ cup) plain flour

Salt & ground black pepper, to taste

16 small or 8 large (about 1.7kg) osso bucco (veal shin slices)

20g (1 tbs) butter

1 tbs olive oil

185ml (¾ cup) dry white wine

2 400g cans whole peeled tomatoes

500ml (2 cups) chicken stock

3 large garlic cloves, roughly chopped

gremolata

⅔ cup chopped fresh continental parsley

3 lemons, rind finely shredded

4 garlic cloves, finely chopped

Pinch of salt

1 Preheat oven to 180°C.

2 Place the flour on a plate and season with salt and pepper. Toss the veal in the seasoned flour to coat, shaking off any excess.

3 Heat the butter and oil in a large, heavy-based ovenproof saucepan over medium-high heat. Cook half the veal for 2–3 minutes each side, until browned. Transfer to a plate. Repeat with the remaining veal.

4 Add wine to pan and stir for 1 minute over high heat. Return the veal to the pan with the tomatoes, stock and garlic, and bring to a simmer.

5 Cover with a lid or foil and cook in preheated oven for 1¾–2 hours or until the veal is very tender.

6 Meanwhile, to make the gremolata, combine the parsley, lemon rind, garlic and salt. Cover and set aside in a cool place until required.

7 Use a slotted spoon to transfer the veal to a bowl. Place the pan over medium-high heat and bring the sauce to the boil. Boil, uncovered, for 10 minutes or until it reduces slightly. Return the veal to the pan and cook for 4–5 minutes or until heated through. Season with salt and pepper, and serve sprinkled with the gremolata.

CREAMY POLENTA

serves: 8   prep: 5 mins   cooking: 35-40 mins

1.75L (7 cups) water

1L (4 cups) chicken stock

500g (3 cups) cornmeal (polenta)

50g (2½ tbs) butter, cubed

100g finely grated parmesan

Salt & ground black pepper, to taste

1 Combine water and stock in a large heavy-based saucepan and bring to the boil over high heat. Gradually add the cornmeal in a steady stream, stirring constantly with a wooden spoon.

2 Reduce heat to low and cook, uncovered, stirring often, for 30–35 minutes or until thick, creamy and pale yellow.

3 Add the butter and parmesan to the polenta and stir until well combined. Taste and season with salt and pepper.

SAUTEED ONION WITH PEAS

picture page 161

serves: 8   prep: 5 mins   cooking: 8–10 mins

60ml (¼ cup) olive oil

2 red onions, halved, thinly sliced

2 anchovy fillets, drained,
   finely chopped

600g (4 cups) frozen peas

2 tsp fresh lemon juice
   Salt & ground black pepper,
   to taste

1 Heat the oil in a medium saucepan over high heat. Add the onions and cook, stirring often, for 5–8 minutes or until they begin to brown. Add the anchovies, reduce heat to medium and cook for 1 minute. (See microwave tip 1.)

2 Meanwhile, cook the peas in a large saucepan of boiling water for 2 minutes, until bright green and tender. Drain. (See microwave tip 2.)

3 Add the peas and lemon juice to the onion mixture and toss to combine. Season with salt and pepper, and serve immediately.

microwave tip 1: place the oil and onion in a medium, heatproof microwave-safe bowl. Cook, uncovered, on High/800watts/100%, stirring after 2 minutes, for 4 minutes or until the onion is soft and light golden. Add the anchovies and heat, uncovered, on Medium/500watts/50% for 1 minute.

microwave tip 2: place the peas in a freezer bag with 3 tsp water and twist the opening to secure. Cook on High/800watts/100% for 2–4 minutes or until bright green and tender.

ORANGE ZABAGLIONE WITH STRAWBERRIES

serves: 8   prep: 5–10 mins   cooking: 10 mins

6 egg yolks

60g (¼ cup) caster sugar

2 tbs orange liqueur (like Cointreau)

750g (3 punnets) small strawberries, hulled, to serve

1 Place the egg yolks and sugar in a large heatproof bowl and use a balloon whisk to whisk until mixture is pale and thickens slightly.

2 Place the bowl over a saucepan of simmering water (make sure that the base of the bowl does not touch the water) and continue to whisk for about 5 minutes or until the mixture is very thick, increases in volume by about half and a ribbon trail forms when the whisk is lifted.

3 Gradually add the liqueur 1 tbs at a time, whisking well after each addition. Continue to whisk for a further 3–4 minutes or until the mixture is very light and frothy, and a ribbon trail forms when the whisk is lifted. Remove the bowl from the pan.

4 Divide the strawberries among serving glasses or dishes and spoon the warm zabaglione over. Serve immediately.

variation: MARSALA ZABAGLIONE WITH FRESH FIGS

In Autumn, try using Marsala instead of the orange liqueur, and serve the zabaglione with 8 quartered or sliced fresh figs instead of the strawberries.

PINK PASSION

SMOKED TROUT PATE
WITH MELBA TOAST

ROAST TURKEY BREAST WITH HERBS

TOMATO & BASIL SALAD

CUCUMBER, PEA & ASPARAGUS SALAD

POTATOES WITH CREAMY
RED-WINE VINEGAR DRESSING

LAST-MINUTE CHRISTMAS PUDDING

BRANDY BUTTER

SUGAR BISCUITS

*Why not try the classic Aussie Christmas drink—
sparkling burgundy? Among the best producers are
Seppelt Great Western and Andrew Garrett*

STRESS-FREE CHRISTMAS

*This is the menu you've been looking for—
a simple, hassle-free solution to festive feasting.
It is filled with traditional touches and
modern twists that bring together the best
of the summer season.
You'll have no trouble putting this entire menu
together on the day itself (even the Christmas
pud!). Alternatively, if you have time, start the
day before—just leave the preparation and
dressing of the salads close to serving.*

PINK PASSION
*Add a generous pour of Campari to a glass of ice, then add a shot of good vodka
followed by plenty of freshly squeezed ruby or yellow grapefruit juice.*

SMOKED TROUT PATE WITH MELBA TOAST

picture page 165
serves: 10   prep: 15 mins   cooking: 15–20 mins
The Melba toast will keep in an airtight container for up to 1 week.
The pâté can be made up to 1 day ahead—keep in an airtight container in the fridge.

10   slices white bread, crusts removed
1   whole (about 330g) smoked rainbow trout
150g   fresh ricotta
85g   (⅓ cup) sour cream
1   green shallot, trimmed, sliced
2 tsp   chopped fresh dill leaves
1½ tbs   fresh lemon juice
   Salt & ground black pepper, to taste

1   Preheat oven to 160°C. Use a rolling pin to roll the bread slices until as thin as possible. Cut each slice into 4 triangles and place on 2 large baking trays. Bake in preheated oven, turning halfway through cooking, for 15–20 minutes or until light golden and crisp. Set aside to cool.

2   Remove the head and skin from the trout and discard. Carefully remove the flesh from the bones and discard the bones.

3   Place trout flesh, ricotta, sour cream, green shallot, dill and lemon juice in the bowl of a food processor. Process until smooth. Season with salt and pepper. Spoon into a serving dish and serve with toast.

ROAST TURKEY BREAST WITH HERBS

serves: 10   prep: 15 mins (+ 10–15 mins resting time)   cooking: 1 hour 10 mins

1   large (about 1.5kg) double turkey breast
2 tsp   olive oil
   Salt

herb sauce
1   bunch parsley, leaves picked
1   bunch basil, leaves picked
3   garlic cloves
125ml   (½ cup) olive oil
125ml   (½ cup) fresh lemon juice
   Salt & ground black pepper, to taste

1   Preheat oven to 180°C.

2   Fold the turkey breast in half and tie with white kitchen string to secure. Place on a wire rack in a roasting pan. Brush the skin with the oil and rub with a little salt. Add enough water to the roasting pan to cover the base by about 1cm.

3   Roast in preheated oven for 1 hour 10 minutes or until the juices run clear when pierced with a skewer at the thickest part. Remove from the oven, cover with foil and set aside for 10–15 minutes to rest.

4   Meanwhile, to make sauce, place the parsley, basil, garlic, oil and lemon juice in the bowl of a food processor. Process until well combined and herbs are finely chopped. Season with salt and pepper. Place in a jug or bowl and cover with plastic wrap until required.

5   Carve the turkey and serve with the sauce.

TOMATO & BASIL SALAD

serves: 10   prep: 10 mins

5   vine-ripened tomatoes, cut into thin wedges
¼ cup   small fresh basil leaves
3 tsp   olive oil
3 tsp   balsamic vinegar
   Salt & ground black pepper, to taste

1   Place the tomatoes and basil in a serving bowl and toss to combine.

2   Drizzle the tomatoes with the oil and vinegar, then sprinkle with salt and pepper. Serve immediately.

CUCUMBER, PEA & ASPARAGUS SALAD

serves: 10   prep: 20 mins   cooking: 5 mins

2 bunches asparagus, diagonally cut into 8cm lengths

500g fresh peas, shelled

1 telegraph cucumber, halved lengthways, thinly sliced

100g baby spinach, washed, dried

mustard dressing

1½ tbs olive oil

1½ tbs white wine vinegar

2 tsp wholegrain mustard

Salt & ground black pepper, to taste

1 To make the dressing, place the oil, vinegar and mustard in a small jug and whisk until well combined. Season with salt and pepper, to taste. Set aside.

2 Bring a large saucepan of water to the boil over high heat. Add the asparagus and peas, and cook for 1–2 minutes or until the asparagus is bright green and tender crisp, and the peas are tender. (See microwave tip.) Drain and transfer to a large bowl of iced water to refresh until cold. Drain well.

3 Place the asparagus, peas, cucumber and spinach in a large serving bowl. Add the dressing and toss well. Serve immediately.

microwave tip: wash the asparagus and place in a freezer bag, adjusting until they are 1–2 deep when the bag is laid flat. Twist the opening to secure. Cook on High/800watts/100% for 2–3 minutes or until bright green and tender crisp. Wash the peas and place in a freezer bag. Twist the opening to secure. Cook on High/800watts/100% for 1–1½ minutes or until tender.

POTATOES WITH CREAMY RED-WINE VINEGAR DRESSING

picture page 167

serves: 10   prep: 10 mins (+ 1 hour cooling time)   cooking: 25–30 mins

30 (about 2kg) pink fir apple, kipfler or chat (small coliban) potatoes

½ bunch green shallots, trimmed, thinly sliced

creamy red-wine vinegar dressing

2 egg yolks

2 tbs red wine vinegar

250ml (1 cup) olive oil

Salt & ground black pepper, to taste

1 Place potatoes in a large saucepan and cover with plenty of cold water. Cover and bring to the boil over high heat. Reduce heat to medium-high and cook, uncovered, for 20 minutes or until just tender. Drain and set aside for 1 hour or until cooled. (See microwave tip.)

2 To make dressing, place egg yolks and vinegar in the bowl of a food processor. Process to combine. With motor running, add oil in a thin, steady stream until combined and thick. Season with salt and pepper.

3 Place potatoes in a serving bowl, add half the dressing and the green shallots, and toss to combine. Serve remaining dressing separately.

microwave tip: pierce each potato 3 times, wash and place on turntable (in layers if necessary). Cook on High/800watts/100% for 5 minutes, then turn and cook on High/800watts/100% for 5–8 minutes or until firm but tender. Place in a large bowl, cover with foil and stand for 10 minutes. Uncover and cool.

LAST-MINUTE CHRISTMAS PUDDING

serves: 10   prep: 10–15 mins (+ 10 mins standing time)   cooking: 3¼ hours

I just love this pudding—it is one of the best I have come across. It is from a friend of mine, Sarah Young, who manages Crackenback Cottage Restaurant and Crackenback Farm Mountain Guesthouse, near Thredbo, New South Wales. It is perfect for people with busy pre-Christmas schedules, who don't have time to think about the pudding until the last minute—it can even be made on the day. The square 60cm calico cloth in which it is cooked is not lined with flour in the traditional way. As a result, the pudding will only last for up to 4 days in the fridge after the initial cooking, which means you almost have to leave it until the last minute! You can soak the dried fruit and dates overnight in 60ml (¼ cup) dark rum or the spirit of your choice for an extra kick.

85g	(½ cup) blanched almonds
300g	(2 cups) plain flour
1 tsp	mixed spice
½ tsp	ground nutmeg
½ tsp	ground ginger
200g	(1 cup, firmly packed) brown sugar
1	375g pkt mixed dried fruit
85g	(½ cup) pitted dates, chopped
500ml	(2 cups) milk
40g	(2 tbs) butter
1 tsp	vanilla essence
2 tsp	bicarbonate of soda
	Icing sugar, to dust
	Brandy butter (see recipe below)
	and/or vanilla ice-cream, to serve

1   Preheat oven to 180°C. Spread the almonds over a baking tray and toast in preheated oven for 8–10 minutes or until golden brown. (See microwave tip.) Remove from the oven and roughly chop. Set aside.

2   Sift the flour, mixed spice, nutmeg and ginger into a large bowl. Add the almonds, sugar, mixed dried fruit and dates, and stir to combine.

3   Place the milk and butter in a saucepan and bring to the boil over medium heat. Remove from the heat, add the vanilla essence and bicarbonate of soda, and stir well. Add to the fruit mixture and stir well. (The pudding mixture will be quite wet, but don't worry, it will be fine.)

4   Place a square 60cm piece of calico on a work surface and spoon the pudding mixture into the centre. Gather the cloth up around the mixture and tie tightly with white kitchen string to seal (leave a space of about 3cm above the mixture for expansion during cooking).

5   Add enough water to a large saucepan to reach a quarter of the way up the side, and bring to the boil. Add the pudding (the water should reach halfway up the side of the pudding). Cover with a lid and boil over medium heat for 3 hours, adding more boiling water if needed.

6   Transfer the pudding to a plate and set aside for 10 minutes. Carefully peel away the calico, turn onto a plate and decorate as desired. Cut into slices and serve dusted with icing sugar and accompanied by the brandy butter and/or ice-cream.

microwave tip: place the almonds in an oven bag and twist the opening to secure. Cook on High/800watts/100%, gently shaking the bag every minute, for 2–3 minutes or until aromatic and lightly toasted.

tip: if you aren't going to eat the pudding on the day it is made, hang it from a cupboard door until it is cold and then transfer to the fridge. To reheat, boil the pudding for 45 minutes (using the method above).

BRANDY BUTTER

serves: 10   prep: 10 mins (+ 2–3 hours chilling time)

My mum makes brandy butter every year to serve with our Christmas pudding. Quite often, she has to hide it at the back of the fridge to stop it from disappearing before the actual day. This brandy butter will keep in the fridge for up to 1 week. A good variation on this recipe is to replace the brandy with an orange liqueur like Cointreau or Grand Marnier.

185g	butter, at room temperature, cubed
1	orange, rind finely grated
80g	(½ cup) pure icing sugar
80ml	(⅓ cup) brandy

1   Use electric beaters to beat butter and orange rind in a medium bowl until pale and creamy. Gradually add icing sugar, beating until fluffy. Gradually add the brandy, beating on low speed until combined.

2   Spoon the brandy butter down the centre of a 40cm-long piece of foil. Wrap the foil around the butter and shape into a log about 30cm long. Twist the ends of the foil and place in the fridge for 2–3 hours or until firm enough to slice.

3   Cut into slices and serve with Christmas pudding.

SUGAR BISCUITS

makes: about 25   prep: 10 mins   cooking: 15–18 mins

These biscuits will keep for up to 1 week in an airtight container.

125g   butter, at room temperature, cubed
80g   (⅓ cup) sugar
¾ tsp   vanilla essence
1   egg yolk
150g   (1 cup) plain flour
1 tbs   sugar, extra, for sprinkling

1   Preheat oven to 160°C. Line 2 baking trays with non-stick baking paper.

2   Place the butter, sugar and vanilla essence in the bowl of a food processor and process until pale and creamy. Add the egg yolk and process to combine. Add the flour and process using the pulse button, scraping down the side of the bowl when necessary, until the mixture just begins to come together.

3   Turn the mixture onto a lightly floured surface and bring together with your hands. Knead lightly until smooth.

4   Use a lightly floured rolling pin to roll half the dough until 5mm-thick. Use a 5cm fluted cutter to cut out the dough and then place on the lined trays. Repeat with the remaining dough. Sprinkle the biscuits with the extra sugar.

5   Bake in preheated oven, swapping the trays halfway through cooking, for 15–18 minutes or until pale golden and cooked through. Remove from the oven and set aside on the trays until cooled completely.

menu for 20

MANGO DAIQUIRI

LIME CRAB SALAD ON
CRISP WONTONS

VIETNAMESE PORK BALLS WITH GREEN
CHILLI DIPPING SAUCE

FRESH CORN &
SWEET POTATO CAKES

LAMB & DIJON BRUSCHETTA

RICH CHOCOLATE TARTLETS

SPARKLING WINE &
STRAWBERRY JELLIES

---

*Sparkling white and red wine is perfect for any
cocktail party. Try the new groovy-looking pigeon
pair of Yellow and Red from Yellowglen*

COCKTAILS

*Finger food doesn't need to be time-consuming
or fiddly to prepare. It should be simple
but impressive, easy yet smart. The trick is
to serve some cold or room-temperature
bites along with some hot ones, and a sweet
treat, if you like. Interesting textures and
flavour combinations are paramount.
Remember, keep it simple, do as much
preparation as you can beforehand and
let your friends lend a hand—your party is
bound to be a success.*

MANGO DAIQUIRI

serves: 4   prep: 10 mins

2	ripe large mangoes, peeled, flesh chopped, frozen
200ml	white rum
100ml	orange liqueur (like Cointreau)
75ml	fresh lemon or lime juice
30ml	vodka (optional)
1	egg white
	Crushed ice
4	small fresh mint sprigs, to decorate

1 Place the frozen mango flesh, rum, orange liqueur, lemon or lime juice, vodka (if using) and egg white in a blender. Add enough crushed ice to fill.

2 Blend until smooth. Pour into glasses and decorate with the mint. Serve immediately.

VIETNAMESE PORK BALLS WITH GREEN CHILLI DIPPING SAUCE

pictured opposite

makes: about 50   prep: 30 mins   cooking: 20–25 mins

90g (1 cup) breadcrumbs, made from day-old bread
60ml (¼ cup) milk
2 lemon grass stems, pale section only
1kg pork mince
6 green shallots, trimmed, thinly sliced
4 garlic cloves, crushed
1 bunch coriander, leaves and stems finely chopped
1 fresh green chilli, deseeded, finely chopped
1½ tbs fish sauce
1 tsp palm or brown sugar
Peanut oil, for cooking

green chilli dipping sauce
125ml (½ cup) rice vinegar
2 tsp fish sauce
1 tsp brown sugar
1 fresh green chilli, thinly sliced

1 Place the breadcrumbs in a large bowl. Add the milk and set aside for 5 minutes or until all the liquid is absorbed.

2 Meanwhile, to make the dipping sauce, combine the vinegar, fish sauce, sugar and chilli in a small bowl. Cover and set aside.

3 Remove the outer layers of the lemon grass, then finely chop. Add to the soaked breadcrumbs with the pork, green shallots, garlic, coriander, chilli, fish sauce and sugar. Use your hands to mix until well combined, then roll into walnut-sized balls and place on a tray.

4 Preheat oven to 180°C. Line 2 baking trays with non-stick baking paper.

5 Add enough oil to a large frying pan to reach 0.5cm up the side, and heat over high heat. Add a third of the pork balls, reduce heat to medium and cook for 3–4 minutes, turning occasionally, until browned. Use a slotted spoon to transfer to the lined trays. Repeat with the remaining pork balls.

6 Cook the pork balls in preheated oven for 10 minutes or until cooked through. Serve warm with the dipping sauce.

LIME CRAB SALAD ON CRISP WONTONS

picture page 175

makes: 40   prep: 20 mins   cooking: 3–4 mins

The wonton wrappers can be cooked up to 1 week before serving and kept in an airtight container. You can make the crab salad up to 1 hour before serving—cover and keep in the fridge.

20 round flour wonton wrappers, halved
1 tbs peanut oil, for brushing
1 small red capsicum, deseeded
1 Lebanese cucumber, quartered lengthways
500g cooked fresh crabmeat, well drained
⅔ cup finely shredded fresh mint leaves
Salt, to taste

dressing
80ml (⅓ cup) fresh lime juice
1½ tbs fish sauce
1 tbs brown or palm sugar
Ground black pepper, to taste

1 Preheat oven to 240°C.

2 Brush wontons lightly with oil on both sides. Place on 2 baking trays. Bake in preheated oven for 3–4 minutes or until golden and crisp.

3 To make the dressing, place the lime juice, fish sauce, sugar and pepper in a screw-top jar. Shake well to combine.

4 Cut capsicum into 5cm-long, thin strips. Thinly slice cucumber. Combine capsicum, cucumber, crabmeat, mint and dressing in a bowl, and toss. Taste and season with salt. Top wontons with crab salad, to serve.

LAMB & DIJON BRUSCHETTA

makes: 40   prep: 30 mins (+ 15 mins resting time)   cooking: 20 mins

The toasted bread slices can be made up to 1 week ahead and kept in an airtight container. The mayonnaise can be made up to 5 days ahead—keep in the fridge. Cook the lamb up to 1 day ahead, cover with foil and keep in the fridge. Return to room temperature just before assembling.

1½ loaves Turkish bread (about 50cm long)

Olive oil, for brushing

Salt & ground black pepper, to taste

3 large garlic cloves, halved

850g (about 12) lamb fillets

160g (1 punnet) snow pea sprouts, ends trimmed

dijon mayonnaise

2 egg yolks

1 tbs Dijon mustard, or to taste

1 tbs fresh lemon juice

200ml olive oil

1½ tbs finely snipped chives

Salt & ground black pepper, to taste

1 Preheat oven to 200°C. Trim the ends of the bread and then cut into portions about 7cm wide. Halve each widthways, then split to make 40 portions in total. Brush the cut sides of the bread with a little olive oil. Place on 2 large baking trays, sprinkle with a little salt and toast in preheated oven for 8 minutes or until light golden. Rub the cut side of each slice with the cut side of a garlic clove. Set aside.

2 Meanwhile, to make the mayonnaise, place egg yolks, mustard and lemon juice in the bowl of a food processor. Process to combine. With the motor running, gradually add the oil in a thin, steady stream until the mayonnaise thickens. Transfer to a bowl and stir in the chives, salt and pepper. Cover and place in the fridge until required.

3 Preheat a large non-stick frying pan or chargrill over high heat. Brush lamb with oil. Reduce heat to medium-high. Cook half the lamb for 3 minutes each side for medium or until cooked to your liking. Place on a plate and set aside for 15 minutes to rest. Cook remaining lamb.

4 To assemble, thinly slice the lamb across the grain. Place the toasted bread on serving platters and top with about 10 snow pea sprouts, 3–4 slices of lamb and a small spoonful of mayonnaise. Sprinkle with black pepper and serve.

FRESH CORN & SWEET POTATO CAKES

picture page 176

makes: 45   prep: 30 mins   cooking: 30 mins

These cakes can be cooked up to 2 days before serving. Keep in an airtight container, layered between pieces of non-stick baking paper, in the fridge. To reheat, place on baking trays lined with non-stick baking paper in an oven preheated to 180°C for 10 minutes or until heated through.

2 corn cobs, husks and silk removed

500g orange sweet potato (kumara), peeled, cut into 2cm chunks

125ml (½ cup) vegetable stock

140g (⅔ cup) couscous

1½ tsp ground cumin

1 tsp ground coriander

¼ tsp sweet paprika

1 bunch coriander, leaves picked, chopped

Salt & ground black pepper, to taste

2 eggs, lightly whisked

90g (½ cup) cornmeal (polenta), for coating

Peanut oil, for frying

2 400g containers natural Continental-style yoghurt

1 Use a sharp knife to remove corn kernels from cobs. Bring a large saucepan of water to the boil. Add corn and sweet potato, cover and return to the boil. Uncover and cook over high heat for 8-10 minutes or until sweet potato is tender. Drain and place in a large bowl. (See microwave tip.) Use a potato masher to roughly mash until mixture begins to come together. Set aside for 10 minutes to cool slightly.

2 Meanwhile, bring stock to the boil in a small saucepan. Remove from heat and stir in couscous. Cover and set aside for 3 minutes or until liquid is absorbed. Use a fork to separate grains. Transfer to a bowl. Add cumin, ground coriander, paprika, fresh coriander, salt and pepper. Toss to combine. Add to corn mixture with eggs, and mix to combine.

3 Place cornmeal on a plate. Shape about 1 tbs of mixture into a patty about 1cm-thick. Roll in cornmeal to lightly coat. Place on a tray lined with non-stick baking paper. Repeat with remaining mixture.

4 Add enough oil to a large non-stick frying pan to reach 0.5cm up the side. Heat over medium-high heat. Add a quarter of the patties and cook for 2 minutes each side or until golden. Drain on paper towel (cover to keep warm if serving immediately). Cook remaining patties, adding more oil to pan if needed. Serve with yoghurt for dipping.

microwave tip: wash the corn kernels and place in a medium microwave-safe bowl. Cover with a lid or plastic wrap, and cook on High/800watts/100% for 3 minutes or until tender. Drain. Wash the sweet potato and place in a medium microwave-safe bowl. Cover with 2 sheets of damp paper towel and cook on High/800watts/100% for 3-4 minutes or until tender.

RICH CHOCOLATE TARTLETS

makes: 48   prep: 20 mins (+ 30 mins resting, 2–2½ hours standing and 20 mins freezing time)   cooking: 20–25 mins

You can make the pastry cases up to 1 week ahead. The filling can be made up to 5 days ahead—keep in an airtight container in the fridge. Set aside at room temperature until soft enough to spoon into the cases just before serving.

225g (1½ cups) plain flour
35g (⅓ cup) cocoa powder
45g (¼ cup) icing sugar
150g butter, chilled, cubed
60ml (¼ cup) iced water
Cocoa powder or icing sugar, to dust

chocolate filling
200ml thickened cream
200g good-quality dark chocolate, finely chopped
40ml (2 tbs) Marsala or liqueur of your choice

1 Place flour, cocoa, icing sugar and butter in the bowl of a food processor. Process until mixture resembles fine breadcrumbs. With the motor running, add water and process until mixture just comes together. Turn onto a lightly floured surface and bring together with your hands. Knead lightly until just smooth. Shape into a disc and wrap in plastic wrap. Place in the fridge for 30 minutes to rest.

2 Meanwhile, to make filling, heat cream in a saucepan over low heat until almost simmering. Place chocolate in a heatproof bowl and add cream. Set aside for 1 minute, then stir until smooth. Stir in Marsala and set aside for 2–2½ hours or until a thick, spoonable consistency.

3 Use a floured rolling pin to roll half the dough on a lightly floured surface until 3mm thick. Use a round 5cm fluted cutter to cut 24 circles. Ease into two 20ml (1 tbs) patty case trays to line. Prick bases twice with a fork and place in the freezer for 20 minutes. Preheat oven to 200°C.

4 Bake the tartlet cases in preheated oven for 10–12 minutes or until cooked through. Remove from oven and set aside for 5 minutes to cool slightly, then turn onto a wire rack to cool completely.

5 Repeat with the remaining pastry to make another 24 tartlet cases.

6 Use a teaspoon to spoon a generous amount of filling into each tartlet case. Serve dusted with cocoa or icing sugar.

SPARKLING WINE & STRAWBERRY JELLIES

serves: 20   prep: 20 mins (+ overnight setting time)   cooking: 10 mins

1.75L (7 cups) water
550g (2½ cups) caster sugar
1 lemon, juiced, strained
2 750ml bottles sparkling wine (like Seaview Brut)
40ml (2 tbs) strawberry liqueur (like Seagram's)
45g (¼ cup) powdered gelatine
5 sheets silver leaf (see note), to decorate

1 Place 1.375 litres (5½ cups) of water in a large saucepan. Add the sugar and lemon juice, and stir over medium heat until the sugar dissolves. Bring to the boil over high heat. Reduce heat to medium and simmer, uncovered, for 5 minutes. Remove from heat and set aside for 5 minutes to cool slightly. Stir in sparkling wine and liqueur.

2 Meanwhile, bring the remaining 375ml (1½ cups) water to the boil in a small saucepan over high heat. Remove from heat and sprinkle with the gelatine. Stir to dissolve and then set aside for 3 minutes or until the mixture is clear. Add to the wine mixture and stir well.

3 Place twenty 180ml Champagne flutes on a tray. Pour the jelly mixture into a jug and then pour into the glasses. Cover each loosely with plastic wrap and place in the fridge overnight to set.

4 Just before serving, use a small, clean paintbrush or tweezers to tear the silver leaf into pieces and place on the jellies to decorate.

note: silver leaf is edible. It is available from good art suppliers, some Indian grocery shops and some good kitchenware stores.

OYSTERS WITH LEMON SOY DRESSING

CROSTINI WITH SARDINE & CAPER PASTE

ROAST SALMON

ROAST ASPARAGUS, PANCETTA
AND PARMESAN SALAD

BABY POTATOES

CRUSTY BREAD

CHEESE PLATTER

CHOCOLATE CELEBRATION CAKE

At a wedding, you definitely need some bubbles, a white and then a red with a spiritual feel. Start with a good Australian sparkling wine, like Hardys Sir James Vintage. Move on to a St Helga Riesling and then a St Huberts Cabernet Sauvignon, and your wedding will be truly blessed

WEDDING

A romantic wedding reception at home with a small, intimate group of friends and family is truly special. This menu is perfect for either a lunchtime or evening affair. Sip bubbles accompanied by oysters and canapés, enjoy the delicate flavour of fresh salmon, and indulge in a chocolate cake like no other. Your guests will love this menu for its uncomplicated elegance and you will adore it for its ease and realistic approach to catering for a crowd.

OYSTERS WITH LEMON SOY DRESSING

picture page 183

makes: 50   prep: 10 mins

The lemon soy dressing (minus the caviar) can be made up to 2 days before serving. Keep in a sealed jar in the fridge.

Rock salt, to serve

50   oysters in half shell, chilled

lemon soy dressing

100ml   fresh lemon juice

1 tbs   soy sauce

1 tbs   olive oil

1 tsp   sesame oil

2 tsp   good-quality caviar

1   To make the lemon soy dressing, place the lemon juice, soy sauce, olive oil and sesame oil in a small screw-top jar. Shake to combine.

2   To serve, spread the rock salt over a serving platter and sit the oysters on top. Add the caviar to the dressing and shake gently. Spoon a small amount of dressing over each oyster and serve immediately.

CROSTINI WITH SARDINE & CAPER PASTE

makes: 64   prep: 10–15 mins   cooking: 20–30 mins

Crostini will keep in an airtight container for up to 1 week. The paste can be made up to 2 days ahead—keep in an airtight container in fridge.

10   115g cans good-quality sardines in oil, drained

12   small (about 35g) drained anchovy fillets

1½   150g jars capers in vinegar, undrained

125ml   (1½ cups) double cream

½   bunch continental parsley, leaves roughly chopped

Ground black pepper, to taste

Fresh continental parsley leaves (optional), extra, to garnish

crostini

4   30cm baguettes (French sticks), cut into 1.5cm-thick slices

Olive oil, for brushing

1   Place the sardines, anchovies and undrained capers in the bowl of a food processor. Process until smooth. Add the cream and parsley, and process until just combined. Season well with pepper.

2   To make the crostini, preheat oven to 160°C. Line 2 baking trays with non-stick baking paper. Brush both sides of the bread slices lightly with oil and then place in a single layer on the lined trays. Cook in preheated oven, swapping the trays halfway through cooking, for 12–15 minutes or until light golden and crisp. Remove from the oven and transfer to wire racks to cool. Repeat with the remaining bread slices.

3   To serve, place a spoonful of the paste on each crostini and garnish with the parsley leaves. (Alternatively, spoon the paste into a serving bowl, place on a platter and arrange the crostini around the bowl.)

ROAST SALMON

serves: 20   prep: 10 mins   cooking: 8–10 mins

You can roast the salmon up to 4 hours ahead. Cool, cover loosely with plastic wrap and keep in the fridge. Serve at room temperature.

3   1kg salmon fillets, skinned, deboned (ask your fishmonger to do this), cut into 20 even portions

1 tbs   extra virgin olive oil
Sea salt (or freshly ground rock salt)
& ground black pepper, to taste
Lemon wedges, to serve

1   Preheat oven to 200°C. Line 3 large baking trays with non-stick baking paper. Cut an extra piece of baking paper for each tray.

2   Place the salmon on the lined trays, 1cm apart. Drizzle with oil and sprinkle with salt and pepper. Cover with the extra pieces of baking paper and roast in preheated oven for 8–10 minutes for medium or until cooked to your liking. Allow to cool with the paper on top.

3   To serve, place salmon and lemon wedges on a large serving platter.

ROAST ASPARAGUS, PANCETTA & PARMESAN SALAD

serves: 20   prep: 15 mins   cooking: 22–25 mins

You can roast the asparagus, pick the parsley leaves and make the dressing up to 1 day before serving. Keep in separate airtight containers in the fridge. The pancetta can be prepared up to 4 hours before serving—cover with foil and set aside.

10   bunches (about 100 spears) asparagus, washed, ends trimmed

2 tbs   olive oil
Salt & ground black pepper, to taste

15   slices pancetta, rind removed

150g   piece parmesan, shaved

1   bunch continental parsley, leaves picked

lemon & olive dressing

80ml   (⅓ cup) canola oil

1½ tbs   olive paste

1 tbs   red wine vinegar

1   large lemon, rind finely grated
Salt & ground black pepper, to taste

1   Preheat oven to 200°C. Line 3 large baking trays with non-stick baking paper.

2   Spread the asparagus over the lined trays. Drizzle with oil and sprinkle with salt and pepper. Cook in preheated oven for 12–15 minutes or until the asparagus tips wilt slightly. Transfer to a large bowl.

3   To make the dressing, place the oil, olive paste, vinegar, lemon rind, salt and pepper in a small screw-top jar. Shake well to combine.

4   Place the pancetta in a single layer on 2 of the lined trays. Cook in preheated oven for 10 minutes or until crisp. Remove from the oven and set aside on paper towel to drain and cool completely. Break the pancetta into pieces.

5   To serve, add the pancetta, parmesan, parsley and dressing to the asparagus, then toss gently to combine. Arrange the salad on a serving platter to serve.

BABY POTATOES

serves: 20   prep: 5 mins (+ 30 mins cooling time)   cooking: 25–30 mins

50   (about 3.5kg) chat (small coliban) potatoes

1 tbs   olive oil
Salt & ground black pepper, to taste

1   Place the potatoes in a large saucepan of cold water. Cover and bring to the boil over high heat. Boil for 15 minutes or until the potatoes are tender when tested with a skewer. Drain and refresh under cold running water. Drain well, then place in a large bowl.

2   Add the oil, salt and pepper to the potatoes and toss gently to combine. Set aside for 30 minutes or until the potatoes have cooled to room temperature. Cover and place in the fridge until required. Return to room temperature before serving.

CHEESE PLATTER

serves: 20   *picture page 188*

For your cheese platter, try a selection of cheeses, such as about 400g blue cheese (like Tasmanian Heritage Fresh True Blue or Gippsland Blue), about 300g cheddar (like King Island Surprise Bay Cheddar or Bega 19th Century Cheddar), about 100g ashed goat's cheese (like Hellenic Cheese Farm Ash Chevre or Edith's Cheese) and about 200g triple-cream white mould cheese (like King Island Dairy Crème de la Crème). Serve the cheeses accompanied by shredded wheatmeal biscuits or oatcakes, pumpernickel bread, slices of baguette (French stick), muscatels and fresh dates.

CHOCOLATE CELEBRATION CAKE

serves: 20   prep: 1½ hours (+ 3 hours standing and 3 hours chilling time)   cooking: 1½ hours

*Make the filling for this wonderfully rich cake when you are ready to assemble it. The cake will keep, either assembled or as
separate layers, wrapped in plastic wrap, in the fridge for up to 4 days before serving. If you would like to freeze any leftovers, wrap well
in plastic wrap and then foil, and place in the freezer for up to 3 months. Defrost either in the fridge or at room temperature. To decorate
the cake, you will need a ribbon (we used satin) about 5cm wide and 1 metre long, and flowers of your choice.*

Melted butter, for greasing
500g good-quality dark chocolate, chopped
500g butter, cubed
160ml (⅔ cup) water
6 eggs, at room temperature
335g (1½ cups) caster sugar
300g (2 cups) self-raising flour
70g (⅔ cup) cocoa powder

ganache
300g hazelnuts
400g good-quality dark chocolate, finely chopped
300ml thin cream
2 tbs Frangelico or brandy

1 Preheat oven to 160°C. Brush a deep, square 23cm cake pan
with the melted butter to grease. Line the base and sides with
non-stick baking paper.

2 Place 250g of chocolate, 250g of butter and 80ml (⅓ cup) of water in
a medium saucepan. Stir over low heat until smooth. Remove from
the heat and set aside to cool slightly. (See microwave tip.)

3 Use electric beaters to whisk 3 eggs and 165g (¾ cup) of sugar in
a large bowl until the mixture thickens slightly. Use a wooden spoon
to gently stir in the chocolate mixture. Sift 150g (1 cup) of flour
and 35g (⅓ cup) of cocoa over the chocolate mixture and stir
gently until combined.

4 Pour the cake mixture into the prepared pan and use the back
of a spoon to smooth the surface. Bake in preheated oven for
40–45 minutes or until crumbs cling to a skewer inserted in the centre
of the cake. Set the cake aside for 10 minutes before turning onto a
wire rack to cool completely.

5 Repeat steps 1–4 to make another square 23cm cake with the
remaining chocolate, butter, water, eggs, sugar, flour and cocoa.

6 To make the ganache, increase the oven temperature to 180°C.
Spread the hazelnuts over a baking tray and cook in preheated oven
for 8–10 minutes or until aromatic. Rub the hazelnuts between a
clean tea towel to remove as much skin as possible. Roughly chop the
hazelnuts and set aside. Place the chocolate in a heatproof bowl.
Place the cream in a small saucepan over medium heat and bring just
to a simmer. Pour the hot cream over the chocolate and set aside for
1 minute. Stir until smooth. Stir in the Frangelico or brandy. Transfer
two-thirds of the ganache to a separate bowl. Stir the hazelnuts into
the remaining ganache. Set both mixtures aside, stirring occasionally,
for about 1 hour or until both are a thick, spreadable consistency.

7 To assemble the cake, place a cake layer on a serving platter or tray.
Spread the hazelnut ganache over the top. Place the other cake layer
on top. Spread the reserved plain ganache over the sides and top of
the cake to coat. Smooth the surface and set aside in a cool place for
1 hour, until the ganache is firm. Cover with plastic wrap and place in
the fridge for at least 3 hours.

8 To serve, cut a strip of non-stick baking paper the same width and
length as the ribbon. Wrap the baking paper around the cake and
secure with a small piece of masking tape. Wrap the ribbon over the
baking paper (this will help keep the ribbon clean) and secure with a
dress pin. Decorate with your choice of fresh flowers. Serve at room
temperature, cut into small portions.

microwave tip: combine 250g of chocolate, 250g of butter and
80ml (⅓ cup) of water in a medium, heatproof microwave-safe bowl.
Heat, uncovered, on High/800watts/100%, stirring every minute,
for 3–4 minutes or until smooth.

WINING & DINING

WITH STUART GREGOR

While there are no set rules for matching food and wine, there are a few tricks that can bring a new dimension to dining in. Remember, though, there is no such thing as a wrong match. If you like it, stick with it, and keep the rules for the road.

There is one steadfast and indisputable rule when it comes to matching food and wine, and it is *not* to never drink red wine with fish or white wine with red meat. No, it's much more fundamental than that—put simply, if you enjoy it, do it.

If you fancy drinking Grange with fish and chips or delicate riesling with a T-bone steak, who am I to say you're on the wrong track?

We have people telling us all the time what to do and what not to do. The last thing you need is another set of rules just when all you want to do is go home, cook a nice meal and have a drink.

But while there are no rules, there is a pretty loose set of guidelines that just might help you along the way.

The first thing to do is to have a good look at the old 'red with red and white with white' rule. While it may seem simplistic and a bit old-fashioned, there is something to be said for this wise old generalisation.

It is a simple fact that most white wines are lighter than most red wines, and that most meals made with red meat tend to be heavier then those made with white meat or fish.

Think about the first thing you do when a piece of fish or seafood is put in front of you. Chances are, you'll reach for a lemon wedge and squeeze it everywhere. (If you're like me, some will squirt in your eye as well, but I think that signals a problem with my technique.)

The lemon adds a bit of acidic freshness to the seafood—a bit of zing and liveliness. Thus, I don't reckon it's a bad idea to have a similar sort of wine, one with a bit of lively freshness and some zing of its own. The best bets would be a young riesling or sauvignon blanc, both of which are naturally quite high in acid and tend to be delicious with any sort of seafood.

And what about oysters and Champagne (or sparkling wine, as we have to call the Australian style now)? Well, I reckon it is a match made in heaven—the creamy, salty oysters and the lively freshness of sparkling wine—in my mind, you could live on that combination alone.

If we move from fish to chicken, we come to a slightly more vexed area because chicken can be many things to many people, not to mention cooked in many ways. A delicate poached chicken breast is very different to a classic roast or even a chicken casserole. So, the key here is to think not of the colour but to match the weight of the wine with the weight of the dish.

If you are making a hearty casserole, whether it be with chicken or beef, you should choose a hearty wine—if you feel like white, try a rich, buttery chardonnay, and if you feel like a red, try a spicy shiraz.

If you are cooking a classic red-meat dish, like roast lamb or beef, or doing your best work on the barbecue, I am going to suggest you think of a few things before choosing your wine.

Firstly, if you are having a roast with lots of vegies and gravy, it makes sense to have a wine with plenty of flavour that is not overwhelmed by the food. Try a robust cabernet sauvignon, or a softer cabernet–merlot blend if you want to be a bit gentler on yourself. As for the barbie, the texture of a chargrilled steak is a perfect match for a rich young shiraz with plenty of tannin (that's the stuff that makes your mouth dry and makes red wine taste a little bit bitter).

Remember that red wine should be served at normal room temperature, not at 35°C. If it is hot and you are outside, whack it in the fridge for half an hour or so to get it back to a decent temperature. And, while we are on a sacrilegious note, under no circumstances should you feel a heathen by putting ice cubes in your white wine. It's practical, lowers the alcohol and doesn't make the wine taste too different. Tell your snobby mates to keep their opinions to themselves—and tell them I told you it was cool.

While I am giving out such sage advice, I should probably tackle the issue of cheese and wine. The best bet with cheese is to match the chalkier, cheddar cheeses with red wine and the softer, creamier cheeses with white wine. Again, don't think about the colour, think about the weight of the cheese and the wine.

While wine has many friends in the world of food, it also has a couple of enemies. They are mainly foods with weird flavours and those with the capacity to coat your tastebuds, rendering the wine's flavours imperceptible.

Among the 'weirdo' foods are flavours like asparagus and artichoke, which can make wine taste a little metallic. Sometimes this is because these foods often come with a bit of vinegar, wine's natural enemy. 'Bad' or 'off' wine tastes like vinegar, so vinegary food makes your wine taste a bit crook.

The other foods you should treat with caution are seemingly harmless but can be quite mischievous. One is the humble egg. The old googy has a very distinct flavour that is often difficult to complement with wine. A runny googy also coats your tongue, making it hard to taste anything at all. If you are going with lots of eggs, try a dry sherry, which is also pretty weird but really tasty and strong enough to fight off the yolk. Another hard-to-match food is chocolate. Its rich, unctuous flavour overwhelms most wines, with the exception of rich unctuous types (surprise, surprise) so try a muscat or tokay from north-east Victoria.

INDEX

INDEX

INDEX

INDEX

ACKNOWLEDGMENTS

Many thanks to my gorgeous husband Paul and beautiful daughter Brooke, for their endless support and for keeping me smiling; to Michelle for her incredible enthusiasm and for being there, through thick and thin—without her, this book wouldn't exist; to Yolande for her wonderful artistic talent and foresight; to Will for always producing such edible images; to Amber for her visual inspiration and being my personal sounding-board; to Anna for her commitment to perfection; to Janelle for her vast knowledge of all things microwave; to Stuart for sharing a drink or two with us all; and the Text team—Patty Brown, Marijcke Thomson, Lesley O'Brien, Melanie Ostell, Aspasia Comino, Alison Turner, Jan Purser and Chong—for their invaluable support and advice.

ACKNOWLEDGMENTS

ADDITIONAL RECIPES

Janelle Bloom
15 (chilli pork & Asian greens stir-fry), 23, 63,
64 (carrot & cabbage salad with orange tahini dressing),
80, 82, 140, 142 (potatoes with persillade),
170 (brandy butter)

Annette Forrest
80, 82, 126

Stuart Gregor
164, 174

Yael Grinham
39, 40, 74 (figs wrapped in prosciutto), 108, 152,
156 (citrus & mint tea), 184, 186

Amber Keller
15 (lychees in lemon grass & mint syrup), 76

Michelle Lawton
90 (steamed water chestnut, spinach & mushroom
dumplings), 119

Jan Purser
5 (chicken & spinach burgers), 16, 53, 98, 100, 102, 154

Dimitra Stais
6, 34 (orange & lemon granita), 44 (lamb pot roast with
mushrooms & rosemary), 124 (red pork curry with
eggplant & basil), 144, 146, 148

Alison Turner
5 (raspberry parfait), 9 (lettuce wraps), 13,
19 (broad bean & garlic pasta), 21 (strawberry &
papaya salad), 24, 92, 120, 128, 131, 132

Frank Urizar
50 (prawn, asparagus & dill salad), 112,
180 (sparkling wine & strawberry jellies)

Sarah Young
170 (last-minute Christmas pudding)

ADDITIONAL PHOTOGRAPHY

Chris Chen
81, 82, 83

Louise Lister
77, 127

Mark O'Meara
5, 8, 12, 13, 21, 24, 25, 37, 38, 41, 52, 93

John Paul Urizar
cover, 4, 17, 19, 20, 49, 73, 79, 112, 113, 175, 176,
177, 179, 181, 187, 190, 191

ADDITIONAL STYLING

Kristen Anderson
17, 138 (tea light), 139, 141, 184

Marie-Hélène Clauzon
19, 20, 45, 79, 112, 113, 175, 176, 177, 179,
181, 187, 190, 191

Yael Grinham
5, 8, 12, 13, 21, 24, 25, 37, 38, 41, 52, 73, 81, 82,
83, 93, 129, 130, 131, 132, 133, 151, 152, 153,
154, 155, 156, 157, 183, 185, 188, 189

Michelle Noerianto
54, 55, 57, 58, 59, 94, 95, 96, 97, 158, 159, 161,
163, 164, 165, 167, 168, 169, 171, 172, 173

Frank Urizar
4, 49, 127, 174, 180

STOCKISTS

Accoutrement (02) 9969 1031
Acorn Trading (02) 9518 9925
Basic Essentials (02) 9328 1227
Country Road Homewear (03) 9267 1400
Dinosaur Designs (02) 9698 3500
Domestic Pots (02) 9386 4099
Empire Homewares (02) 9380 8877
EQ:IQ (02) 9231 4922
Orson & Blake (02) 9326 1155
Papaya (02) 9362 1620
Peppergreen (02) 4877 1488
Ruby Star Traders (02) 9518 7899
Shack (02) 9960 5718
The Bay Tree (02) 9328 1101
Wheel&Barrow Homewares (02) 9413 9530

ABOUT AUSTRALIAN GOOD TASTE

Author Anneka Manning is the Food Editor of australian good taste *magazine.* australian good taste *is filled with simple-to-make recipes; fresh, useful ideas; and features about Australians and the issues that affect them. It is a lifestyle manual that puts easy, affordable living within everybody's reach.*

A recent addition to the good taste *family is the* good taste collection, *a beautiful series of user-friendly books also edited by Anneka and designed to sit side by side with* australian good taste *in your kitchen.*

If you don't own good food, *Anneka's first cookbook, you can pick it up at selected bookshops.* australian good taste *and the* good taste collection *are available through Woolworths, Safeway, Purity, Roelf Vos and BIG W stores. For information about the magazine or to order the* good taste collection *or* good food, *please call (02) 9952 4611. You can also find us on the Woolworths website:* www.woolworths.com.au/agt

To subscribe to australian good taste *magazine, follow the prompts at the above web site or call our subscription hotline on 1300 361 344.*

Lesley O'Brien
Editor, australian good taste